AN AWAY GAME EVERY WEEK

Memories of Bristol Rovers

AN AWAY GAME EVERY WEEK

Memories of Bristol Rovers

Ray Kendall

breedon **books**

PUBLISHING

First published in Great Britain in 2001 by
The Breedon Books Publishing Company Limited
Breedon House, 3 The Parker Centre, Derby, DE21 4SZ.

ISBN 1 85983 249 0

Printed and bound by Butler & Tanner, Frome,
Somerset, England.

Jacket printing by GreenShires, Leicester, England.

CONTENTS

INTRODUCTION

THIS is my story, and the story of Bristol Rovers Football Club. The two have been intertwined in my life for more than 50 years, and I couldn't tell the one tale without the other.

It is the story as I remember it. I must acknowledge the help I've had from checking statistics and team line-ups from Mike Jay's excellent book *Bristol Rovers A Complete Record 1883-1987*. Another book *Pirates in Profile*, which Mike Jay also compiled along with Stephen Byrne, has also been a huge help in refreshing my memory.

However I have tried mostly to stay away from facts and figures and recall the people who have been important down the years, because they are the most essential part of any club. I wanted to catch the special atmosphere of Rovers, who must always have been one of the most friendly clubs in the League.

There are probably some people who should have been included who have been missed out. To them I apologise. And if my memory has let me down in the accuracy of any of the stories, I'm sorry for that too.

I'm so thrilled at being given the opportunity to tell the story of my life. And I hope you will enjoy reading it even half as much as I have enjoyed living it.

Ray Kendall

GROWING UP

THE Gas. My very first memories start there. Long before I ever got involved with Bristol Rovers, long before I was even interested in football.

My first home was in Jubilee Row, just off Lower Ashley Road, near to the site of the old Eastville Stadium. Then we moved to Good Hind Street with my grandparents. The M32 cuts right through that area now on a giant flyover, but you can still see beneath it the remains of the old terrace houses that were home to a close knit and friendly community.

The biggest landmark then was the giant gasometer, which rose and fell according to the season over at the back of the old Eastville Stadium, near to His Majesty's Cinema. If you grew up there you couldn't mistake the old, sweet smell of the gasworks. It was a sort of sickly scent that wafted across the area and got into everything.

Once a fortnight it was my job to go across the old stadium car park and head off to the gasworks, together with my brother Arthur, to collect the coke that was needed to keep the house heated for another couple of weeks.

In those days the well off burned coal, and the rest of us had to make do with coke – the coal that had already been used by the company to get the gas out and leave us with the leftovers. We had to walk up there, pay our deposit to hire a cart and a couple of sacks, then push it back down to home.

It's funny how your childhood memories always stay. I've got a vivid picture in my mind of myself at the age of about seven or eight, holding one handle of the cart while Arthur held the other, struggling to get half a hundredweight of coke back to our house without the cart falling over. Then one of us – and it seemed as if it was usually me – had to push the empty cart and sacks back up the hill to get our deposit money back.

About all you can see of those days now is the old Eastville Social Club at the back of IKEA's great car park. And to be honest all the football ground really meant to me when I was that little was a handy short cut through to the gasworks with that great heavy cart.

Of course when World War Two began, football was of even less consequence to us. Rovers shut down during the war, and the ground became just a giant bowl surrounded by corrugated iron fencing to keep inquisitive kids like me out of it.

That was a time that tested families. And we had our fair share of the dramas and catastrophes that those six years brought.

My Mum came from a big family, with five sisters, so I had loads of cousins and later nephews and nieces. We're spread right through the West Country now.

But my close concerns then were with my older sister Marge, ten years older than me, Arthur who was two years older, and my little sister Jean who was born a year later than I was, which, by the way, had been on 28 October 1929.

Good Hind Street had it's own street air raid shelter, where 16 or 17 of us would crowd in for the night after the sirens went off to wait for the all clear. The area was a target for the German bombing, close to the munitions works at Bretnall Dolman and Rogers, and the raids would start at 6pm and not stop until six the next morning. Mr Dolman, incidentally, was Bristol City chairman for many years and it's well recorded that he only went to Ashton Gate because he had wanted to be on the board at Rovers but was turned down by the other directors. Anyway, it is generally recognised that Bristol took one horrific raid when it seemed the whole city was bombed, and Good Hind Street was one of the places to feel the worst.

We were literally buried in the shelter for four hours after it took a direct hit. One fellow, whose name was Harry Weekes, died because he had his back to the wall and got caught in the full blast. The rest of us just spent ages wondering if we were ever going to get out.

When we did it was to a scene of devastation. The road was full of craters, the houses – including ours – had been destroyed. It had been such a friendly community. Four shops on the corners, a newsagents called Dunks, Allens who sold sweets, Weekes the bakery where poor Harry had worked, and a fish and chip shop with an Italian name I could never pronounce. And in the space of a few hours it was all gone. We had been lucky to get out alive, and that incident will live in my memory forever.

We went first of all to Claremont Street, where 14 of us had to sleep in one room. We were then allocated a property to move into by the side of Bath Bridge – only for that to be blown sky high by another bomb the night before we were due to move in.

So we went to 39 Church Road in Horfield. Ironically, for the way my football story was going to work out, I'd gone from the edge of the old Rovers ground to just up the road to what would become the new one at the Memorial Stadium. I didn't know that then.

We were almost out of that house before we were in it, though. On the very first night we moved in it was hit by a land mine, which showered the whole house with earth. The mine landed 150 yards from our new home, but the earth landed across all the houses. My poor mum had plenty to do in any case trying to clean and organise a different house, and she now had all the windows covered with mud.

We were luckier than most, because we all survived the conflict. The closest we came to a direct loss was because there hadn't been enough room in the shelter for Marge on the night our house got hit. She was in bed in one room – and a great beam fell across the bed in the room next to it. Fortunately she didn't know anything about it. My Dad had fought in World War One and was too old to see active service again. He – like most of the men left at home – did his duty as a fire watcher. And with the women working in the munitions factories, most of the time we kids were left to fend for ourselves.

It was a frightening time. Horrific, really. But somehow you got used to that side of it and instead it just became exciting. We would sit on the roof of the shelter in Claremont Street at times and watch the sky lit up by the fires from the anti-aircraft guns and tracers. And you could hear and feel the giant gun at Purdown – known as Purdown Percy – which seemed to shake the entire city of Bristol every time it boomed into the dark night.

At weekends we had parties, parties like you've never known and that probably will never happen with the same sort of carefree moods again. Nobody knew what the next day might bring, so people simply lived for the moment they were in.

Arthur and I used to have the job of clearing out all the furniture in the house to make room for everybody when it was our turn to be hosts. We were just old enough to be involved in everything and catch the atmosphere, drama and excitement.

I learned to dance. At the age of 13 I went to Morris's School to learn how to jitterbug and bop, and I loved going out around all the different dance halls. Each district had a dance in the Church Hall on different nights, and we were out three or four times a week to enjoy the fun.

It was another world, really. Things were part of everyday life that have simply disappeared. Like going to the pawn shop every Monday with my Grandad's Hunter watch and then fetching it back again on Friday so he could wear it at the weekend. I don't think he ever knew how much money we could get for it!

Or the ritual of washday Mondays, when the clothes had to be boiled and then – on wet days – hung down the passage dripping wet with newspapers on the floor to try to mop up the water.

Once we'd gone to Horfield I went to Ashley Down Boys School – and more particularly joined Ashley Down Boys Club. A wonderful man called Les Jones ran it, and that was where I began to catch the football bug.

I believe my Dad was a good footballer. He was a cobbler, a little short feller, but before the war he had played for Cardiff City as a tricky outside-left. And Arthur was also a good player – in fact he had trials for Rovers after the war and was offered a contract. But he could make more money as a printer at a company called Mardon Son and Hall, and so turned it down.

Me? Well Ashley Down Boys club helped me fall in love with all sports. We played tennis, table tennis, snooker, darts – and especially football. And that was where my love affair with Bristol Rovers all began.

FIRST STEPS
IN FOOTBALL

IN the years I was at Rovers, every game was an away match, with skips to prepare to move all the gear from a training ground to an HQ. And really my first football experiences were ideal to prepare me for that.

I was 12 or 13 years old when I started playing for Ashley Down Boys Club at Eden Grove, in games on Horfield Common on a Sunday afternoon. Now coming, as I did, from a reasonable Church-going family, that gave me a problem or two. Mum and Dad weren't too keen because Sunday was a day for putting on your best suit and your best behaviour.

So I used to tell them I was going to a mate's house, and then sneak my football kit off with me and change when I got there to go and play.

The Boys Club was so well organised. We had proper football kit to play in, which was quite an event back then. On Saturdays our matches were at Eden Grove and well organised, while Sundays on the common were more for fun.

To be honest I was never all that good as a footballer. As I said my Dad had been a good player, and my brother Arthur was offered pro terms, but somewhere the genes never quite got passed on! The nearest I got to playing for a living was after the war when I started playing for Horfield Sports – although even then I never got in the first team.

A fellow called Fred Capel and his son used to run it, and he was also in charge of an engineering works in Yate on the outskirts of Bristol. Those of us who were in the football team on Saturday used to get the chance to earn some extra money the next day by going into his works and doing all the cleaning. He'd pay a couple of quid for us to sweep up all the rubbish that collected on the floor during the week, and that was quite a bonus for anybody then. It was quite a perk for being in the team. But if Arthur had the chance to make a real living out of being a footballer and turned it down, that opportunity would never happen for me. I simply wasn't good enough.

So really I gradually got into watching football, drifting very slowly towards Rovers.

In the wartime they hadn't been playing. I don't know why, but Eastville was just a giant, neglected bowl. The dog racing, speedway, all of that came later.

Daft as it might seem, it was Bath City that was the place to go to watch football in those days. Of course they did used to get decent games and teams over at Ashton Gate, because many of the soldiers who were stationed at Salisbury Plain used to turn out for Bristol City. I went there a few times, but it was at Twerton Park that my real education began.

In the wartime you never knew who was playing until you turned up. The sides were drawn from whichever players happened to be in the district, and because Bath was close to so many military bases they used to turn out unbelievable sides. We had to travel by train to get there, getting off at Oldfield Park Station to join the rest of a huge throng making their way on the short walk to Twerton Park.

I can remember seeing Laurie Scott and George Hardwick, the two England full-backs, in tandem for Bath City. And Stan Mortensen, the great inside-forward who was a mainstay of England sides with Stan Matthews and Tom Finney right through into the 1950s, used to play regularly for Bath.

They also had the first black chap I ever saw play football, a chap called Paris who was a Bournemouth player. He was serving at Warminster and regularly appeared at Twerton Park. I think that Clyde Best of West Ham is often credited as the first black player, but in my mind he was a couple of decades behind Mr Paris!

When you later saw Twerton Park when Rovers played there, it seems incredible the size of crowds that could be packed in during those times. But I saw Bath play Aston Villa in the wartime FA Cup with more than 20,000 in there. And Villa had a superb team, with Wakeham in goal, and Potts, Cummings, Massey, Broome and Houghton who were all international players at that time.

It was after the war when Bristol Rovers started up again, and they were always going to be my team. It was a question of where I lived, and you simply couldn't support anybody else. I had started working during the war at the Willis tobacco factory in Bedminster as a 14-year -old and I can remember massive arguments between the Rovers and City fans. I don't suppose it's changed now!!

The first game I saw at Eastville was against Newport County. I don't know the score. I can just recall the sight of hundreds and hundreds of people walking from every direction to get there. From the Muller Road, from Stapleton, Staple Hill, Whitehall, Speedwell, from all over the city. The place was alive with people coming to see the game.

And there were all sorts of activities that went on beforehand on the pitch. Don't ask me who organised it or how, but there would be dog shows, brass bands, or fire service demonstrations, with crowds of 25,000 to 30,000 crammed in to enjoy the entertainment. The giant Tote Board for the dog racing dominated one end of the ground, while the other was just an earth bank. You got to know the same people, who stood in the same spot week in and week out.

I'm not sure I can remember any games or results from just after the war – but I can recall a few of the players. In goal was Jack Weare, who was 6ft 2ins tall and always wore the sort of flat cap which was fashionable then. Harry Smith was one of the full-backs. And there was a little inside-forward known as Baggy Whitfield.

Now Mr Whitfield – whose real name was Wilfred – got his nickname because of the incredibly long shorts he liked to wear underneath his blue and white quartered shirt. He was only a small man, and his shorts went right over his knees while his huge thick shin pads seemed to go right up his legs in the opposite direction. This was before the stormwater tunnel was built at Eastville and the pitch was always a quagmire. So by the time Baggy's boots had disappeared six inches or so into the mud, he didn't seem to have any legs at all!

The biggest memory of Rovers in those days was that Gasworks smell. I had grown up with it, of course, but returning to football matches used to make it a special aroma that belonged only to the club. It was like a dry odour, with something rich about it, like a farmyard smell gone wrong. And you always knew when the gasometer was working because it would be at different heights. In the week the coal would all come into the railway sidings by Stapleton Road station. By Saturday it was being turned into gas and the distinctive, rich smell would waft across the pitch.

To be honest I was still only an occasional Rovers fan at this time, so I can tell you far more about my own history than I can the club's. I know that the ground had been sold to stave off a financial crisis, which I think was why it was shut down during the war. But I was more interested in following the players than the club.

At times we would catch a train up to Birmingham to visit either Villa Park or Birmingham City. I can remember seeing England's two goalkeepers Sam Bartram and Gil Merrick at opposite ends of one match at St Andrew's. When Charlton got a penalty, Bartram ran the length of the field to take it – and then went dashing back again after he hit the bar and Birmingham threatened a breakaway. We used to stand at the railway line end of St Andrew's, where the soot from the steam trains as they chugged through behind the stand would get in your eyes and make them red raw.

At about this time I had damaged my arm badly, and I actually started work with it in a cradle-type sling. I did it at the boys club, falling awkwardly as I tried to jump from an old fashioned vaulting box. I landed in a heap with both bones of my right arm forced through the skin just below the elbow. They rushed me off to the BRI, and from there I got moved to Winford to see a specialist. His name was Mr Priddy – and he was recognised as one of the top specialists in the West Country. To my horror – and that of my parents, his verdict was that the arm would have to be amputated. My parents actually signed the consent form to have the operation done, and I went to hospital prepared for the worst.

My luck was in. Dr Priddy took a surprise day off, and left a wonderful lady called Dr Betty Fox in charge. And she decided she could do something better for me and she saved it. I'm not sure – with all the lifting and carrying – that I could ever have been a kit man if she hadn't!

Anyway I started work at Willis as a page boy, with my arm still in a cradle, running messages around the factory. That was a good job then, and gradually I was moved into the cutting room and on into the cigarette-making rooms where all the ladies were running the machines while their menfolk were off fighting at the front. We produced 350 Woodbines a minute.

I landed up doing virtually everything in the factory that required a speaking voice, as the union rep and on the factory council to listen to everybody's moans and groans. We met once a month with the management to go through all the grumbles – and I was actually on that council alongside Bristol's current Lord Mayor Graham Robertson. He was a very "affluent" speaker, using phrases and terminology that I had never come across before.

At 18 it was time for National Service, and I set off to join up with the RAF at West Kirby near Liverpool. If the war seemed tough, that was nothing compared to going away from home for the first time. And I hated service life at first – you were treated like shit during 18 weeks of marching, and learning how to polish boots and scrub this and scrub that. It was known as square bashing, all done at the double up, and I loathed every minute.

It also took me away from Nancy, the girl from round the corner in Filton Avenue that I was planning to marry. She had become my special dancing partner on all those evenings when the bands played at Horfield Parish Church, and I set off pledging my loyalty to her.

The one consolation was the chance to get weekend passes to go to Anfield or Goodison Park for football, and then go dancing in the evening at the Grafton Rooms. I still have friends who live on Merseyside and keep me in touch with the football there.

I was two years in the RAF, and even my exit wasn't straightforward. I was serving as a flight mechanic on the Berlin airlift when my demob papers came through, and it took four days on a train before I made it back to Bristol.

That journey seemed to be an epic to last forever. I was on leave in Innsbrück, had to go from there to Hanover, on to Lubec, down to Hamburg and then to the Hook of Holland. An overnight ferry to Harwich was followed by a train to Kings Cross, up to Preston for my papers, and then at last back down to Bristol. It was four days on a train altogether, and I thought it would be the biggest adventure of my life. Little did I know that a 51-year football odyssey was about to begin.

Meanwhile the next shock was to discover that Nancy, bless her, had fallen for an American serviceman and gone off with him. And though I went out with her sister a few times it was never quite the same! I came home planning to marry Nancy – instead I ended up married to Bristol Rovers Football Club!

BROUGH FLETCHER

ROVERS' first manager after the war had a name that sounds now like a character from a cheap romantic story. And I'm sure you'd picture Brough Fletcher as you read it as a tall, handsome, dark and mysterious man.

The truth of the real Brough Fletcher was somewhat different. He was actually a little, tubby man, who was a happy-go-lucky character and friendly with the world. I had begun to socialise in the old Eastville club beside the stadium where he and the players all used to hang around, and that was where supporters like myself got to meet and get to know their heroes.

Brough was a former Barnsley footballer who had been given the job as Rovers manager in 1938 – just in time for the club to be closed down during the conflict! So he worked instead at the aircraft factories at BAC, and when peacetime came was in the right place at the right time simply to pick up where he left off. He had a chap called Cooper as his assistant – although where he came from I don't know – and Bert Williams as the physio. Now Bert was something of a character. As far as I'm aware he had no formal qualifications to be a physiotherapist whatever, but he did have the most enormous hands. They were almost like magic, as he'd rub and massage the injured parts of a player's body and make him feel fit again. He stayed in the job for years and I don't think I ever heard a player or manager unhappy at the treatment they received from those powerful strong fingers. Everybody trusted Bert, and he got on with treating and training the players while Brough Fletcher and Mr Cooper got on with the job of reorganising the club after the war.

And my word there must have been some work to do. Poor Rovers have always been considered to be a bit, let's say, under resourced, and never more so than in those days. I recall them playing against Newport County and Brough had to borrow a ball from Bath City because Rovers didn't own a single football! Those were the days before Mitre gave you a stock of training as well as match balls like they do in the sponsorship era of today!

I recall seeing them preparing to leave for away games, with all their equipment packed up in old Gladstone bags – an old fashioned bag that was about 20 inches long and circular, made of solid leather. Into one of those each player would cram his boots, shirt, shorts, tie-ups, pads and socks. Again it seems an incredible contrast to the modern kit with all the giant skips full of playing and warm-up equipment.

On home match days it seemed the entire city walked to Eastville Stadium for first football and then dog racing, and you had to get there early with your wooden box to stand on to have a chance of seeing the game. Speedway also had a great following, and the giant bowl of the ground seemed so often to be packed with people.

The south side of the ground had an old Victorian wooden stand which seated 1,200 people, with a wooden tower above the roof for the dog racing. To the right from that was the Muller Road bank, a huge concrete mound built with a mixture of earth, concrete and old railway sleepers. The kennels for the greyhounds were just over the back at the Muller Road end, and on a Saturday lunchtime before the game the dogs would be taken out to do exercise. They were then weighed, given the chance to perform their business at the back of the stand, before being put back in their allocated spot in a special kennel area to be ready for racing later. If the gasworks gave a strong smell, I can assure you it was even worse down there!! For all the young players not involved in games on that match day, it left an unpleasant chore. They spent lots of time with water hoses washing down – mainly to stop the dogs' muck being taken into the boardroom, stand and dressing-room areas. If you think that there were always seven or eight racing starts, with six dogs each race, it made it quite a big job for the lads.

The north side had a long, low covered shed with everybody standing, and at the His Majesty's Cinema end of the ground was the Tote End, covered by the huge roof with an elaborate scoreboard system full of complicated charts to help the greyhound punters work out their bets.

The most unique thing about Eastville were the flowerbeds behind each goal, lovely banana shaped beds that were always full of colourful blooms. Somehow even in the depths of winter there seemed to be something always growing, and it made the ground quite uniquely picturesque.

On the perimeter wall at the Tote End could be found Brough Fletcher's office, a shed about 15 feet by 20 feet in which four people worked. You used to have to go there to get tickets.

Brough had his own little office within it along with the assistant manager Mr Cooper, while Bert Williams did all his healing down in the South Stand where the dressing-rooms were. The office was completed by Walter Jenning, the chief scout, and his assistant, Ernie Wood, who found good players from all over the West Country, and John Gummow, the secretary.

John used to organise all sorts of people to do voluntary jobs. That was how Rovers was run then, and the same sort of spirit of everybody helping for the love of the club has stayed since. There were lots of things that needed to click into place on a matchday, and John was quite efficient at organising it all.

You forget how complicated it could be to sort out jobs that are so simple now. One man named Bill Pinnell had the responsibility of getting the half-time scores, and had to ring on a crackly old phone to the Press Association in London to have them read to him. I often stood near him as he took the scores down, and he used to listen intently and go furious if anybody made a noise and he couldn't hear! We used to play him up. I would call out the scores to others behind the bar, and he would yell at me: "Get out". Especially everybody always wanted to know the Bristol City score and would cheer if they were losing just as he tried to hear the next result from London!

The club's chairman was Con Stevens with his vice chairman John Hare. Con, who also owned the dog tracks at Wimbledon and Oxford, co-opted other directors to help get the club going again. There was a man called Philip Hort who was in the hotel business, another called Hampton Allpass and a Dr Nicholas who was the medical minister for the West Country. Then secretary John Gummow was a big influence on everybody and seemed to organise everything.

Mind you, John was a strange man, for all his ability to get things done. When Rovers were winning you could always see him parading around the ground, walking proudly down the dog track area. He used to love to be in the limelight. But I'm sorry to say that when the team were losing it was a different story – you couldn't find him! He'd stay inside that little portable hut on the perimeter wall, tucked against the galvanised fencing that surrounded the whole ground in those days.

The only other office was a small one at the back of the South stand where Ron Moules, the assistant secretary, used to work, near to all the dog racing club staff who were formed into a separate company.

When you look now at the magnificent pitches at Premiership grounds, and even at the smaller stadiums, it seems incredible to think about the condition of the Eastville pitch then. It was some years before they built the Stormwater tunnel at a cost of around £1m, and until then whenever the River Frome rose it simply flooded the pitch. And I mean flooded – often up to three quarters the height of the goalposts. In fact Ronnie Moules was known to go to work in his little office by swimming from one side of the ground to the other!

I could dig out the record books for the results from those Division Three South days, but I don't know how much they would mean to you or me. I remember more the atmosphere than the specific games. But I do know that things began to go wrong for Brough, and instead of going out to put it right with new talent he just closed in and vegetated. Because of that by 1949 there was a board meeting to discuss the state of the playing side of the club.

Brough didn't even wait to hear the verdict of the directors, instead choosing to go to the Eastville club for a drink. Once the meeting was over, and the decision was taken, the directors had to send a messenger up the Fishponds Road where Brough had a house and put his notice through his door after the board meeting was over. He was to claim later that he was never told verbally that he had been sacked.

But sacked he was – and the decision was to give the job to Bert Tann who had been brought in as a coach around 18 months earlier.

It was probably the most significant appointment in Bristol Rovers' history, because Bert began an era that made the club unique…

THE BERT TANN ERA

THE man who was to mould Bristol Rovers could not have come with a higher recommendation. For it was none other than Sir Stanley Rous, the top man at the FA and later the inspiring force behind the creation of FIFA, who was behind his appointment.

Con Stevens, as well as his interests in dog racing and his farm at Easton-in-Gordano on the northern edge of Somerset, owned the Wimbledon Motor Company. And it was there that one day Sir Stanley called in to discuss buying himself a new car. Their conversation turned to football, and Sir Stanley suggested that if Con wanted to appoint an up and coming coach he should go to this chap Tann who was a player at Charlton.

That happened some 18 months before the end of Brough Fletcher's reign, and it probably gave Bert Tann just enough time to take a good look at the club and form his ideas.

And his ideas were revolutionary, I can tell you. It amuses me to see now that football clubs are investing heavily in coaching schoolkids, while trying to go into the community through schools and getting their players to visit hospitals. Bert Tann brought all those ideas into action 50 years ago.

To give yourself a picture of the man, he was tall and imposing – about 6ft 2ins which in those days was an exceptional height. He must have weighed about 12 stone, and kept himself extremely fit. If you've seen pictures of Anthony Eden, the Prime Minister who took Britain through the Suez crisis, imagine him without his moustache and that would give you an idea of Bert's appearance. Or should I say Mr Tann, because that was how he expected everybody to refer to him. There was no calling of directors by their first names in those days – and Mr Tann expected everybody to address him with respect as well.

The air about him was unbelievable. He radiated authority and class. And his clothes were magnificent – all high fashion tailoring from Regent Street. His shoes were polished to the brightest shine, and his football gear was always equally immaculate. Everything in his life had to be spick and span and just right, and he expected everybody at his club to meet those same standards.

As a person Bert Tann was a strong character who was firm but fair and warm. He would deal with players individually and in private rather than in front of everybody else – and never rollock a team after a game. Down the years I was to see many managers let off their full fury in the dressing-room. I didn't work within those private confines in the early years while Bert was in charge, but I know from all that players told me that he was always quiet and constructive after games. He used to save everything he had to say until Monday, and then he could go through a game in minute detail. He would talk to players sometimes about incidents that happened weeks ago, and would explain them as if it had been yesterday.

Like all the great managers he could say different things to different people, and gently point out both where they had been at fault and what they had done well. Remember he certainly never had the benefit of videos that modern coaches use to analyse a game. Bert Tann simply used his brain and his knowledge, and could be just as detailed as any modern coach with his films and rewind button! He just had that gift. I don't think he was a great player with Charlton Athletic but he must have done well with all the coaching things.

You have to remember that Bristol Rovers had sold Eastville Stadium just before the war to Con Stevens for the princely sum of £12,000 to save the club from bankruptcy. Dog racing had gradually taken a grip on the club before the war. The Oxford Greyhound Company made numerous attempts to stage events at Eastville, and eventually the potential income it could generate became too much to ignore and it had started in 1932. By 1939 it was a case of the tail wagging the dog, because Rovers had to apply for re-election and with debts of £16,000 and bankruptcy hanging over the club, the then chairman Mr Fred Ashmead – despite fierce opposition – decided to sell the ground. That was a decision, of course, which was to dominate the club's story for decades – and come to that still has a major impact on Rovers now. But it meant that while that particular pre-war crisis had been averted, Bristol Rovers could never be a wealthy club again. So cost saving factors were just as important then as they are now, and it meant Bert's vision was invaluable.

Within a couple of years of taking over he put forward the famous "no buy, no sell" policy which the club followed throughout the rest of his reign. More significant was that at the same time the money saved on transfer fees was pumped into creating a coaching and scouting set-up which was far-sighted and in those days virtually unique. So many players began to be found from all over the country.

The strength of any manager is his staff, and Bert was no exception. He had Fred Ford as his assistant. Fred was a lovely man, who was tall, just like Bert, possibly even taller. And like Bert he had moved down from London with his wife and two boys – who later played for England at rugby.

Fred was formerly assistant manager to the great Bill Shankly when he completely ran Carlisle, so had a superb pedigree. He had a little Austin Seven, in which he went all over the country watching for talent. He would cram himself into this tiny car with his knees pushed up against the steering wheel, and set off at midday after training to go all sorts of distances. He might head off to Derby or

Manchester – and remember this was before the motorways – and yet somehow he was always back in the club at nine the next morning talking about who he had seen, which players he fancied or which he didn't rate at all. Rovers didn't buy – but any who wouldn't cost any money were jotted down into the system for later signings.

But then that was typical of Bert's attention to detail. And while he could seem an aloof character to those who were outside the club, he was a very caring man to those within it. When I started working at the club taking boys on school tours, Bert would always make a point of seeing them on their journey around the ground and giving them his time. No wonder their little faces would look up at this giant, famous man in awe.

As I said Bert had far-sighted ideas about involving the club in the community. He even roped in two schoolmasters by the names of Arthur Cox and Bert Francis to help organise the links between the club, local schools, and all the other organisations in the area.

The "no buy, no sell" idea was his most famous creation. You couldn't do it now, of course, because players have the freedom to move on at the end of their contracts. But in those days the club effectively owned them, and it meant Bert could dictate their futures in the best possible way.

I think most look back on it as the basis of the club's most successful time, but there was no doubt it was controversial then. Many considered it was simply a sign that the club lacked ambition, and there was lots of criticism. Over the other side of the city at Ashton Gate they were buying players for all sorts of positions, and many Rovers fans wanted their club to do the same. But Bert would quietly point out the times when City spent significant sums of money and got no return – especially there was a winger from Fulham called David Thomas on whom they spent a very big sum but he only played 13 times before he had to pack up because of a cruciate ligament injury, which almost always ended a career in those days.

Within a year or so of taking over, Bert's force of personality had begun to dominate the club so much that while some disagreed with his ideas, people had no option but to go along with them. And in time I think most people, especially the directors, began to believe he was right, and that what many took to be a penny pinching idea was in fact far-sighted and exactly right for Bristol Rovers and its supporters.

I suppose Rovers were doubly lucky in that, at the same time that Bert was creating his vision of how to run a club, Ron Moules was also progressing from assistant to club secretary with a similar sort of imagination and creative ideas. It was Ron who started special trains to football, and who also inspired the Eastville market.

It was Ron who got me involved in the club, of course. It all happened on a day out watching cricket when Gloucestershire were playing Somerset. I don't know why I sat in the particular seat I chose that day, but it was to shape my entire life.

Almost as soon as I had started talking cricket with this chap, and his wife who was sat alongside him, we seemed to click. He introduced himself as Ron, and his wife as Jan, and don't ask me why but within 15 minutes we were chatting as if we had known each other all our lives. And after that he never left me out of anything. Again, don't ask me why. But if he and Jan were going to any social function or party, I was always invited to go along with them. Jan was quite a character, a jolly person who would say her thoughts to anyone or anybody. Ron, who had only just been made assistant secretary at Rovers, asked me if I ever travelled to watch cricket – and I said that to be honest I didn't because of the cost. So Ron and Jan invited me to go with them – together with John Gummow and his lady – to see the Cheltenham cricket festival. To travel by car was a very special event in those days, and Cheltenham too was a wonderful occasion with the billowing white figures of the cricketers against a green and mellow backdrop.

Anyway Ron asked me what I did on Saturdays, and I told him I played football. I wanted to go on playing too, because I saw myself as similar to Billy Wright or Danny Blanchflower. They were my two particular idols, two stylish players who never seemed to get their knicks dirty. I also came off nice and clean from most games –

although while in their case it was because they were so classy, in mine it was just because I was rubbish and didn't get involved enough!!

Ron persuaded me in his inimitable style – the same manner with which he found volunteers for every job around the football club – that my Saturdays would be better spent as a steward at Eastville. And so it was that I first worked for Bristol Rovers in 1950 looking after the supporters and helping them find safe places to stand high up on the terraces, or in the South Stand seating area.

In my view Ron was one of the great administrators of the game. And who knows where he might have ended up in it's history books, either, because I can vividly remember him telling me once how he had gone to Anfield to be interviewed for the job as Liverpool secretary. The previous incumbent had apparently sadly committed suicide in one of the turnstile blocks, due to the pressure of the club going into Europe for the first time. He simply hadn't been able to cope with all the travel and hotel arrangements which in those days was completely unknown territory and not easy to organise. Anyway, Ron was invited to talk about replacing him. They actually offered him the job, but after much agonising he decided to turn it down because of his love of Bristol Rovers. The man who got the job instead was Peter Robinson, who went on to become the Chief Executive responsible for some of that club's greatest days. What a magnificent figurehead for Liverpool he was.

Ron was always ahead of the field, a very thorough man who never missed a detail. I can remember being at his house on a Sunday when he used to tally up all the wages. I'd go to his house in Robertson Road where we would have lunch, play cards with Dave Gray and Eddie Gunton – and then he'd get his work out and settle down to make sure everything was exactly as it should be.

So I started work as a steward, with a man called Jack Neil as the senior man and Bill Blackburn organising us into different positions around the ground. It was a testing job at times – I remember one game where a man pulled a knife at the back of the North Stand. I'd love to tell you of my heroics disarming him, but the truth was I had a policeman with me and he whipped it off this fellow as quick as anything. It went to a court case and caused a sensation that there should have been a knife wielded at a football ground. That was years before the game began to have its hooligan problems.

Eric Godfrey, who was the Supporters' Club chairman, suggested my next job which was to take school parties around the stadium – again one of those revolutionary ideas when it was brought in back then but which is common place at all of the big clubs and stadiums now. They give it a posh name now, the Community Scheme, but it is not really any different to the ideas that Rovers introduced all those years ago.

I used to have to report at midday, three hours before kick-off, to take 20 or 30 boys around the ground. They would come from the big public schools like Millfield or Clifton College as well as from other schools. Eric Godfrey used to organise it all. I simply turned up and took them around.

It was great fun with all the questions and answers, and it certainly suited me. You had to make up a story or two to tell them as we went along. We'd start out in the dressing-room, where I would show them how Bert Williams used to lay out all the kit. It was all neatly hung in number order, with shirt, shorts, socks, tie-ups, boots and a towel for each player, plus polish and brushes and liniment and all the other things that go to make up the preparation for a game. From there we would go into the away room, and on to the referee, and then go right around the ground. At the Tote End the dogs would all be barking in their kennels, where they were waiting for whichever of the seven races they were running in. Then we'd go up the north side of the ground to the Muller Road bank, coming across there carefully because of all the dog muck which had not yet been washed down! Then it would be back to the boardroom in the South Stand, which was a lovely room with a sloping ceiling that had atmosphere and charm. There the boys would be shown the giant portrait of the Duke of Beaufort, who was the club President, and sometimes – especially at night games, they would have the honour of actually meeting the Duke himself. Then their tour finished by going to their free stand seat – complete with a programme – to watch the game with their schoolmasters.

Now that was a privilege, for the Duke was an impressive character. He was even taller than Bert Tann, at about 6ft 4ins, and for all that he was a genuine aristocrat he was one of the most down to earth men I ever met. He was so friendly to everybody, and I would sit the boys down and tell them the history of the football club. I'm sure that must have won us many a new young supporter. Then if the boys were lucky they would return to visit the referee of the day who would give them a short talk. There were many great characters, among them a Roger Kirkpatrick who claimed to be a bell-ringer and sidesman at his local church, as well as telling all sorts of tales and anecdotes, although I'm not sure if any of them were actually true!

The whole atmosphere was friendly and welcoming, and I'm convinced that Bert's "no buy, no sell" policy played a big part in that. I think it brought all the players together as a unit because they had stability and were allowed to develop without the pressure of somebody being bought for big money to replace them. They all earned the same money, and if there were any bonuses to be earned they earned them together. If they achieved anything at the end of the season they also knew they had achieved it together. They were also together seven days a week, and would train together and live together.

That was especially true in pre-season, when Bert always took them to Uphill in Weston-super-Mare. Bill Andrews would allow them to use Weston cricket ground, and for two weeks the football club literally made camp there. They set up a giant marquee for a fortnight, and training consisted of running up and down the sand dunes. I don't know if you've ever done any running, but let me tell you that if you ran in sand dunes you knew you had been training. Your legs ended up like lead.

Ted Osbourne used to do all the cooking and organise the marquee. He took all the stuff down there, and the whole playing staff used to live there for two or three weeks, and were only allowed home at weekends. My job, in contrast, was to travel on the train to

Weston on Saturday and on Saturday and Sunday night to look after the marquee! It was like an Army base, with all the players having to fold their blankets and put them neatly with their pillows every morning. It was an exercise of rigorous discipline. The whole squad slept in the giant marquee, while the staff had separate tents. And if the English summer decided to offer rain instead of sunshine it wouldn't matter – the Rovers camp still went ahead. The one treat was on Saturday when they had beef stew after training for their lunch before they went home. On every other day it was strictly light food – salads and so on – before training in the afternoon again.

During the week they had to run from Uphill to the Knightston Baths, some three miles down to the other end of Weston, and then they had brine baths before running back again. You can imagine what it was like with running shoes on one minute, boots the next, and sweating like a pig the next. The washing used to come back in a hell of a state. But they were all together, and the "no buy, no sell" worked well for each individual as well as for the team.

They shared their failures and their glories – and in the years Bert ran the side there were probably far more of the latter.

A TEAM THAT PICKED ITSELF

WHATEVER problems Bert Tann had to struggle with, picking a team wasn't one of them. Week in, and week out throughout a complete decade in the 1950s you could write down the 11 names who would represent Bristol Rovers.

The record books show that he inherited most of his team, and added just a couple of key players to shape exactly what he wanted. And from there he just let them play together, bond together, and grow together into a side that will always stay in the legends of the club.

You only have to look up the list of the record League appearances at Bristol Rovers to understand the consistency that Tann achieved. An amazing NINE of the top 17 on the list were in the side in his first year in charge.

As I cast my mind back to Tann's first team I can name them one by one, starting with the huge figure of Bert Hoyle in goal. He was a colossus of a man who had been discovered playing for Exeter and signed for the princely sum of £350 as Bert Tann first assessed the areas he needed to strengthen.

Maybe it was because of his wartime experiences serving in Italy, Yugoslavia and Greece. Or maybe he was just a happy man. For whatever reason Bert was one of those people who lived his life to the full. He was always jolly and joking, a hearty, friendly soul who was loved by the fans who flocked to follow post-war football. In fact at one time he happened to mention that he liked oranges, and from then on whenever he ran to the Muller Road bank before a game he seemed to be hit by a barrage of fruit from his admirers.

It was typical of Bert that he always collected them up, and after games would go up to Frenchay hospital and pass them on to other war veterans who had not been as fortunate in leaving the services unscarred.

Bert may have been happy-go-lucky, but was passionate about the game. I remember once seeing him in the tea-room after a match, fuming because Bert Tann had decided to drop Peter Hooper from that day's team and Rovers had lost. He confronted Bert and grabbed him by the throat, holding him up like a gamekeeper would hold a rabbit he'd just caught. And don't forget that Bert Tann was a big man. Bert Hoyle was simply bigger – and quite upset at breaking a winning run of results!

It was a tragedy that his time in goal was ended prematurely. One night in 1953, on his way back to Exeter after keeping a clean sheet against Bristol City, Bert lost control of his car as he went into a double-S bend at Cullompton where the road goes over a railway line on a bridge on the old A38. His car smashed into a parapet of the bridge, and Bert fractured his skull. Poor Bert was in hospital for many months, and never played again.

Sadly he wasn't the only one of Tann's first team to suffer tragedy. At least Bert recovered from his injuries to live a happy retirement running a pub in Devon, but Harry Bamford was not so lucky. The only good fortune for Rovers fans was that by the time Harry became a road crash victim he had totted up an amazing 486 League games.

Harry was a right-back, but played the game like a centre-forward. He thought nothing of dribbling the ball across his own 18-yard box, and he would frighten the fans out of their wits at times with his confident control in tight situations. He was a tall, quiet man – another who had seen active service in the war in Burma – and he loved his wife, his pigeons, his garden and his two daughters. Through all the years he played for Rovers as a full-back I can't remember a single winger getting the better of him – apart, ironically, from a little lad called Sid Williams who played for Bristol City. He was so short, and Harry so tall, that somehow the Rovers man always appeared to get turned inside and out.

His other great love was his motor scooter, and that was how his career was ultimately cut short. One day in October 1958 he had been to coach some boys at Clifton College, and on the way back was involved in a collision with a car, leaving him with injuries from which he ultimately died. The whole city of Bristol came to a standstill on the day of his funeral, and Bert Tann made a moving tribute speech and said a part of Bristol Rovers had died with him.

Yet you can go on through that team and find player after significant player. At left-back was Geoff Fox, who may not figure on the all-time appearance list in the top 20, but still totted up 274 League games. He matched up superbly with Bamford, both of them looking to get forward and pass the ball in days when most full-backs were no more than big, rugged defenders.

Jackie Pitt at right-half was one of Rovers great servants. It's incredible to think he was 26 years old before he made his League debut for Rovers in their first fixture after the war. All the more amazing that he then turned out 467 times. Oh, and then he became the club's groundsman too. He's still to be seen at Rovers matches now.

Jackie was probably my favourite-ever Rovers player. Harry Bamford would run him a close second, but I loved the neat touches as well as the total commitment about Jackie's game. He used to pass the ball with such accuracy, working it forward to George Petherbridge the little winger. Jackie could also take free-kicks with devastating accuracy, picking out the head of Geoff Bradford to supply so many of his goals.

He was fiercely committed and a fiery character, rather than cool and calm like some of the others. I remember seeing him and Bristol City's Ernie Peacock both sent off for fighting with each other during a passionate derby game. Yet I also remember them actually leaving the pitch and going down the tunnel with their arms around each other, embarrassed and feeling foolish at how their anger had got the better of them. He wouldn't be half the player in today's game where the referees are much tougher on bad tackles. I remember Jackie taking on Raich Carter, the great England star, when he was playing for Hull and Carter being upset and needled right from the start.

At centre-half was Ray Warren, a great club captain and a Bristol lad who was a superb header of the ball. Jackie Pitt wasn't the biggest – he was much like Billy Wright – so it was Warren who won the headers and dominated when the ball was in the air. I recall him facing down the years the greats like John Charles, Tommy Lawton and Trevor Ford and never giving them a look-in.

Then there was Peter Sampson at left-half, a quiet, calm footballer who was the perfect accomplice to Jackie's more fiery style.

Once you start talking about forwards, then we're thinking of the legends of the Bristol Rovers story.

On the right wing was George Petherbridge, just 5ft 4ins tall but a box of tricks who could go past defenders and centre the ball with either foot. In fact he was so versatile that he actually played all of the 1952-3 championship season on the LEFT wing because Josser Watling was out of favour.

Josser, incidentally, was the natural comedian of the team. A really funny guy. He always seemed to have a new joke to tell or a ready one-liner to make everybody laugh. I think every successful team needs at least one character like that because you have to have some happiness around the place. The boys need to enjoy being footballers. Josser also played the piano brilliantly, and would get everybody up for a sing song.

Vic Lambden was an exciting forward, all arms and legs and action all the time as he seemed to run all day. And Billy Roost was another Bristolian, a ginger haired lad who might have been better known in the game but for Bert's "no buy, no sell" policy. Liverpool were desperate to sign him and offered big money, but Rovers wouldn't let him move.

Last from that team – but certainly not least – was Geoff Bradford. I mean, 242 goals in 461 League games tell their own story, don't they?

But I suppose that doesn't tell you much about a man with whom I got quite friendly. In fact I'm quite proud to say that, because you must remember that these days were long before I began to work full-time for the club.

Most of them would spend their time around the Eastville club, and it was possible for people like me to get to know them and become their friends. And how you felt honoured to be close to the 11 men who were your heroes, I can tell you.

Geoff was a quiet and unassuming man, who loved to read a good book and was modest about his achievements. I think he was also quietly very disappointed that he never had more of a chance at international level. He often went away with the England squads, together with his friend John Atyeo from Bristol City. But only once did he get a chance to play. It was the era of Stanley Matthews and Stanley Mortensen as the wingers, and with that sort of service Geoff would surely have flourished at centre-forward every bit as much as Tom Finney did.

In all honesty Geoff wasn't one to chase after a ball if he wasn't certain to get it, and maybe his work rate didn't help him at international level. But then again it was also probably the fact that he was playing his football outside the top division which counted against him, and his only cap was in October 1955 against Denmark. Even then he scored the final goal in a 5-1 victory. So quite what else he was supposed to do to win another cap I just don't know.

THE CUP GIANTKILLERS

EVEN now, as you look at the old record books from Bert Tann's time, one result stands out. The FA Cup, 3 January 1956, round three. Bristol Rovers 4, Manchester United 0.

Nobody could convince me that wasn't the greatest day in Rovers' history. If you think of United as dominant as they are now, when the likes of Giggs and Beckham have popstar status, then I can assure it was no different back in that era.

These were the Busby Babes, and while the modern United sides might be tempted to field a few reserves in Cup ties, in those days there was never any question that the strongest possible team would play. Admittedly the great Duncan Edwards was missing with an injury, but otherwise the side that United fielded had all the big names – Woods, Billy Foulkes, Roger Byrne who I idolised, Colman, Jones, Whitefoot, Berry, Doherty, Tommy Taylor, Violet, Pegg. All of them were internationals.

I've got a copy of an old newspaper report which calls it Rovers' finest hour. You couldn't dispute that some 45 years later, could you?

There have been Cup giant killings down the years. But how many have been so emphatic, so complete and utterly convincing? How many have had such a dramatic scoreline?

By this time Rovers, of course, had become a strong team in the old Second Division, building steadily on Bert Tann's management and expertise. The solid base of the side which he laid down in those first few seasons had helped win promotion in 1953, collecting the old Third Division South title after stitching together 12 successive wins in the middle of the season. And on to it he had added some extra names – none more exciting than a raw, powerful teenage centre-forward by the name of Alfie Biggs.

Perhaps I'm getting ahead of myself by talking about the United game, because Bert Tann's era had established its potential in his first season with another historic Cup exploit against the mighty Newcastle. It would surely be wrong to ignore that.

I suppose that was probably the game that really lifted Rovers after the war and captured the imagination completely of the new generation of fans which Tann – and John Gummow and Ron Moules – were working so hard to attract.

Any manager needs some success in his first season to establish a reputation, and Bert couldn't have hoped for a more thrilling set of exploits. A cup run that began with Rovers needing two replays to get past Llanelly, and two more to dispose of Gillingham, hardly signalled the excitement to come. Yet suddenly Aldershot, Luton and Hull had also fallen victim to the growing confidence of Tann's emerging Rovers team, and the club had reached the sixth round – further than they had ever gone before.

When the little balls came from the hat and paired us with Newcastle, the whole city of Bristol caught cup fever. Never mind that the game was at St James' Park, and meant an epic journey from one end of the country to the other. I simply had to be there.

It meant an all-day train journey on Friday, changing at Birmingham, before I eventually reached Blyth where I could expect a welcome at my brother-in-law's house for the night. Then it was on to the game, to squeeze in as part of a crowd of 63,000, almost all stood up on packed terraces. I was lucky, because I could go to the game with Ron and Jan who by now were firm friends.

Newcastle were at that time one of the great sides, with their legends like Jackie Milburn, Joe Harvey and the Robledo brothers. And Rovers' cause was hardly helped when George Petherbridge was injured. But incredibly they held on to achieve a 0-0 draw, and that was when things really hit fever pitch.

The team came back on Sunday, by which time many like myself had come home during the Saturday night into the early hours, and we waited to meet them at the station with a rapturous welcome. There were thousands waiting to greet their heroes – and then thousands more who began queuing to get tickets.

Now you probably would picture the 1950s with this idea of an orderly line of happy men wearing flat hats, patiently waiting their turn. Don't you believe it. There were 100,000 fighting to lay their hands on 24,000 tickets for the replay on the Wednesday afternoon, and there was lots of ill feeling. There were people who had vouchers but could get no ticket. There were people pushing and shoving into the queue. There were lines of policemen fighting to control the crowd and bring back some order.

For three hours a line of policemen, with arms linked, held the bridge over the River Frome against more than 50,000 desperate Rovers supporters who were pushing pace by pace to try to reach the Eastville car park. Inside the car park were 28,000 more, all hoping to get the chance to see the big game. His Majesty's Cinema was turned into a casualty clearing station

When the queue was at its longest, John Gummow toured its full length in a police car, telling the crowd: "There are already enough people in the car park to take all the available tickets and you haven't a chance". But still they all waited in the vain hope of reaching the front.

Ron, Jan and John Gummow were effectively locked in the office for three days, as they tackled together the job of selling tickets and counting money. And then somehow by Wednesday afternoon all the work was done and the game was on.

I was working at Wills, but managed to get the afternoon off to go. What an occasion it was. Jackie Milburn scored early on for Newcastle, but then Geoff Bradford equalised and such a noise I had never known before. Everybody seemed to have rattles and bells, and the whole ground shook. People all took stools which were supposed to be for the kids to stand on, but nine times out of ten they used to stand on them themselves and pass the boys down to the front! The dog track meant that there was a 15ft wide area where all the children could sit, and somehow that all added to the excitement of the day. In the event, of course, Newcastle's greater strength took them through. They won 3-1, and went on to win the FA Cup that season, while Rovers fans were left only to think of what might have been.

Yet the Cup run, while it probably damaged Rovers' promotion hopes that year because the results fell away through a glut of games in March and April, had still sowed the seeds of success for Tann's new team. And by 1953 they were on the march into the Second Division.

Bradford was the hero of that year, collecting 33 League goals while Vic Lambden got 24. Yet it wasn't achieved without its dramas, especially after poor Bert Hoyle had suffered that horrific road crash.

A lad called Howard Radford, who had been discovered playing for a Welsh club called Penrhiwceiber – and don't ask me how to pronounce that – stepped out of the reserves to steer the side to complete their triumph. Or at least that was the plan. Instead, after a 0-0 draw in his first match at Exeter on St Valentine's Day, he kept only one more clean sheet, a 3-0 win against Ipswich Town in March 1953. Bert Tann, growing increasingly frustrated, broke his own "no-buy, no-sell" rule by spending £2,000 on Bob Anderson from Crystal Palace to get through the final agonising few matches. Somehow in the run-in the team lost its confidence, and poor Bert couldn't understand that. He kept imploring them to keep playing in the way they had done all season, but somehow the nerves had taken over. Rovers finally clinched it with a Geoff Bradford hat-trick at home to Newport County – but when I tell you that was the only victory in the final nine League games of the season you'll understand just how tense it all became.

But promotion was achieved, the team were treated to a civic reception – and they shared the princely sum of £275 as their bonus for winning the title. It was split equally among the lot of them.

For the next two years Rovers consolidated their place in the Second Division, twice finishing in ninth place. And Howard Radford, the goalie who had been so nervous when the pressure fell on him in that promotion season, slowly established himself again as Bert's number one. In fact he went on to play 244 League games and was basically first choice until 1962.

The most significant event of the first season in the higher division, however, happened on 6 February 1954. That was the day that Bert Tann decided to give this young, raw boy called Alfie Biggs, who was still two days from his 18th birthday, his debut in a match at Lincoln. As they say, a star was born.

Alfie had come from Knowle, which is really Bristol City territory, and had actually started his career, as far as I'm aware, at Ashton Gate. They didn't really bother with him though, and so he came to Rovers in search of his chance to make it as a footballer. He was a tall lad – about 6ft 1in – with blond hair and a confident air about him. I suppose he was modest in his way, but certainly never backward in coming forward when he wanted to and that attitude shone through from the moment he was first picked for the team. He missed only two games for the remainder of that season, collected his first League goal, and slowly established himself as a favourite.

Alfie, and I'm still quite close to him now so I'm not frightened to say this, loved all the good things in life. He loved being a footballer, and he loved to have a drink, and a joke, and a bet. He'd gamble on billiards, snooker, dog racing, horse racing, playing cards, absolutely anything. If we were away overnight he seemed always to be able to get a bottle with him. Whether it was wine or a beer he enjoyed it, and it never seemed to affect his game. He liked the ladies, as well, and I think the girls were quite fond of him too! Certainly they always seemed to flock around.

In those days after a game the players always went to the Eastville club, where they would enjoy a few sandwiches and some beers to talk about what had gone on. Alfie was a good snooker player too, and would always take on the lads for money. Then he would go out into the city to different clubs to go socialising before eventually finding his way home.

I suppose in these modern days that lifestyle would be frowned on, but it was part and parcel of a footballer's life then. They were just working lads who enjoyed their days and nights and providing they turned up on matchday and produced the goods nobody worried.

And Alfie certainly produced the goods – especially on that momentous day on 3 January 1956 when Manchester United came to Bristol and left with their tails between their legs.

My strongest memory of that day? Well it has to be of United arriving in their motor bus at the Tote End where the players and officials entrance was sited. John Gummow used in those days to send free tickets to the unit of Purdown hospital where patients whose minds had been affected by the war were still being treated, along with others who were mentally ill. It gave them the chance to enjoy some football, while they also did embroidery work and produced souvenirs that would go to the club shop. Again it was a typical case of Rovers and their friendly approach to the community which was being fostered in those times.

Anyway, these poor people were waiting in a line outside the entrance for their turn to get in, while a big crowd were also pushing and shoving for a chance to see the great United stars. The stewards were trying to hold everybody back so the players could get in, and as they stepped down towards the gate I can remember Matt Busby surveying those in the crowd closest to him and saying almost scornfully: "So this is the standard of supporters we have got today"!

It was also my debut that day on the public address system at Eastville, because the fellow who normally did it, whose name was Brian Jones, never turned up. Maybe he got stuck in the crowd, whatever I don't know. I think that he got moved by his company to Blackpool at about the same time so perhaps he had already gone. For whatever reason, Bert Tann said he wanted a West Country voice to take over and I got told to get on with it.

I was a bag of nerves. I followed the patter which Rovers had laid out for me, and welcomed the public and the visiting team, and was then told to announce the players and the goalscorers as they went in. It meant I had to stand behind an old Raymond Glendenning-style microphone, which was suspended by four springs, on the front row of the South Stand, with 35,872 people looking on.

I did get the chance to do a rehearsal earlier in the day and it went okay – and I suppose I can't have been that bad when the match came around either because I ended up doing the same job for the next 19 years! I was on the microphone for first team games, reserve team games, youth team games, just about anything that was staged. And it was an honour eventually to be called "the voice of Eastville".

What a match it was for my first public performance, though. There were just ten minutes gone when Biggs got the first goal, and the noise was deafening beyond belief. They said you could hear the roar when Rovers scored five or six miles away across the town, and I'm not surprised. I just recall the excitement of it all, on a blustery day, watching Bristol Rovers completely destroy the best team in the land. And believe me Rovers put United through absolute murders in all departments from goalkeeper to number 11.

Barrie Meyer got the second just before half-time, and then Biggs made it three in the 62nd minute before Bradford wrapped it all up seven minutes from the end. My memory is that it could have been more but for United's England international goalkeeper Ray Wood – and the press cuttings of the time say the same thing. Desmond Hackett, the legendary football writer of the *Daily Express*, summed it up with the phrase: "Bristol Rovers were the £110 team with the million-dollar touch of class."

At the end there was cheering and clapping, and it was so emotional it was unbelievable. No one even attempted to go on the pitch. They just stood on the terraces and cheered and applauded the greatest football day they had seen – or probably would ever see. United went sadly back by coach to Temple Meads and then by train to Manchester. I had a few beers in the ladies' tea room where the players' wives and girlfriends had their own bar. (Daisy, Bert Tann's wife, used to run it and invariably I was invited in). Then I went out on the town for the night and got drunk out of my mind!

I think we all believed that night we had a team which was ready to go on and win promotion to the First Division, and compete with the likes of United and Newcastle for the real honours of the game. So nobody could have dreamed how the next part of Bert Tann's era would evolve.

IN A BROKEN DREAM

AS the crowds flocked to Eastville, and the fame of the likes of Bradford, Petherbridge, Biggs, Bamford and Sampson grew, so the club began to develop.

We felt important, and certainly I was becoming more and more to feel that, even though I was a part-time volunteer, I was a member of staff. Bert Tann himself looked after me, ringing once on a Friday lunchtime to see if I could get away from work early and join him in London.

He was big friends with Cliff Michelmore the TV personality, and they had been planning to stay together in London during the Football Secretary's and Manager's annual conference. Cliff had let him down at the last minute, and Bert wondered if I'd like to take advantage of the rooms which had been booked.

We stayed in a luxury hotel just off Regent Street, ate the finest food and drank the finest wines, and for me it was a step into a world I had never imagined. I even met Liz Taylor in the hotel corridor – although for once in my life I wasn't brave enough to speak to a stranger so she'll never know! On Saturday we went shopping, and Bert then asked me to go back and collect the overcoat he'd bought. It cost £1,000. And that was in about 1957!

The mood of success and affluence was spreading to the stadium. In 1958 they built the new North Stand, put up in just 14 weeks at a cost of £60,000. It was state of the art stuff, and I remember being reminded by John Gummow to mention on the microphone, and on the school tours, how the seats were on a 28 inches base – and that it was two inches wider than the biggest seats at Ashton Gate! There were floodlights installed in 1959 which were on pylons 146 feet high – again a bit of one-upmanship because that was four feet higher than those at City! Lots of construction work went on throughout the ground. The Muller Road bank was concreted, and so was the Tote End, all to improve the safety.

But what I guess nobody realised was the cost that the club was going to have to pay to meet all these improvements. And just as the original decision to sell the stadium had been in response to a financial crisis, so along came another short term move which was to have long term consequences. The stadium directors were finding it hard to fund all the improvements, and were pressing to get money out of the football club to pay for it. They got their way.

You'll remember that the "no buy, no sell" policy had been broken when Bert Hoyle was injured to achieve promotion. Well now it was broken again in response to debts that were building up from all the construction projects. Only instead of buying to win promotion, this time it meant selling which resulted in relegation.

One day in February 1961, completely out of the blue, came the news that Alfie Biggs had been sold to Preston North End for £40,000. It was a massive transfer fee for those days, but caused uproar among the Rovers fans. Nobody had wanted to lose Alfie – least of all Bert Tann. But he had been told by the board that a player had to be sold to ease the debts, and Biggs was the man who could command the highest fee.

It came at a bad time for Tann, whose team were already growing old together and reaching the point where he would need to change them around. To lose their prolific, folk hero goalscorer was a huge strain. He had also just lost his number two Fred Ford who walked out to manage Bristol City – although more of that later.

Tann brought in a lad from Tottenham called John Hills, who had been on the fringes of their FA Cup-winning team. He arrived with a brand new Triumph Herald, bought for £750, and bragged at how he'd paid cash for it with the proceeds of selling Wembley Cup Final tickets. Suffice to say he didn't last more than seven matches under Bert's strict moral codes.

Perhaps the mood of players was changing, because there were other occasions when Tann's high standards were tested. One such case concerned a Welsh inside-forward called Dai Ward, who had been a regular star throughout the second part of the 1950s. Ward, a tiny man from Barry who stood just 5ft 7ins tall, won a full Welsh cap in a match against England in 1958. He also got a hat-trick in four minutes against Doncaster in one game, as well as scoring in eight successive League games in the spring of 1956. But he was a fiery and headstrong character, and before a match at home to Brighton on New Year's Eve 1960 he got involved in a furious disagreement with Bert over what his tactical role should be. To show his disgust he then went on to the field and refused to perform, at times just blatantly letting the ball roll under his foot and out for an opposition throw-in when it was passed to him. Not surprisingly he never played for Rovers again.

Throughout the rest of the team there were changes to be made and experiments to be carried out, as well. Geoff Bradford even played at full-back while Ray Mabbutt, a smallish man, was tried at centre-forward. For probably the first time in Tann's era he was forced to chop and change his players, using 31 of them in a season and then 24 the next year. Eventually three defeats and two draws in April 1962 doomed them to the drop.

That must have been so hard for Tann to take, to see his side that had been built with such ambition go sliding back to Division Three. He responded by bringing Biggs back from Preston to bolster his attack. And while Alfie was welcomed back as a popular hero, and resumed his goalscoring feats, he was to become a key figure in an even bigger shame that was still to follow.

Howard Radford, the goalkeeper who had been a regular through

244 League games, had reached the end of his days. And so Bert brought in a lad from Middlesbrough called Esmond Million. And he also signed a centre-forward from Plymouth by the name of Keith Williams.

They both looked to be players of great promise. Williams scored on his debut, and followed up with more goals in Division Three. And Million made some fantastic saves with wonderful agility.

And yet... something always seemed odd about both players. Million might make some brilliant saves, but would then throw a goal in with an astonishing error. And Williams would finish one chance with clinical precision and then slice the next one wide from a few yards.

It seemed a mystery to me, and to most of the crowd, but I suppose we just put it down as one of the erratic things that made football unique. And probably the other players felt that way too until the club began sliding closer and closer to the prospect of a second successive relegation year. And then there came a 2-2 draw at relegation rivals Bradford in which Million dropped two horrendous clangers to rob Rovers of victory.

There were harsh words in the dressing-room – but nothing compared to a week later when they went to Ashton Gate and were wiped away 4-1 by the local rivals. Biggs was furious and together with Norman Sykes, a 6ft 2ins super fit centre-half who had emerged as a rock like figure in the previous few seasons, he vowed to find out what was going on.

In an angry scene on Monday the pair of them confronted Million and Williams and accused them of cheating and lacking effort. One was missing goals at one end, while the other was pulling off great saves one minute and then letting easy shots in the next.

It was Million, who was a bit of baby, who broke first. He dissolved into tears in the dressing-room and cried about what he had done. Williams denied it at first, but the truth was out. They had both been trying to rig matches to make money from fixed odds and fixed score betting, and it transpired were part of a much wider conspiracy that took in Bronco Lane, Peter Swan and Tony Kay, along with many more players from all over League football.

Sykes and Biggs told Bert Tann of their suspicions, and he dealt with it superbly. Fred Ford and Bert Williams went with him as witnesses as the two players were confronted and were then immediately suspended by the club. I'm sure nobody would have wanted it swept under the carpet, but Bert wouldn't have allowed that anyway. These were two men who had betrayed their team mates and they had to be handled with full force. It was a scandal that ran across the whole game for weeks, and a source of great shame at Eastville that the story had begun to break from our club.

It was all kept under wraps until Friday, when the story began to trickle out into the national newspapers. And on Saturday I was instructed that I had to introduce Ron Moules to the microphone because the situation was so grave it was felt it had to be told to the Bristol public by a full-time official rather than just a volunteer which I was. It took a period of weeks for the FA to gather the evidence, and I don't think either of them were involved in football again. The same could be said of all the other players throughout the country who were involved in a shocking scandal.

It was a shocking period for us, not only because of the extent of the scandal and the feeling of betrayal, but because we couldn't afford to lose two players. And yet at the same time we couldn't afford to keep them either if they were not giving their best.

It fell to a local lad called Bernard Hall, just 20 years old, to come in as goalkeeper for the remainder of the season, and he performed superbly in a vital match at Halifax which we had to win to stay up.

The crowd for that game was just 2,126 – and 500 of them were from Bristol as the club's supporters rallied around to try to help the team avoid falling into Division Four.

While Hall answered the crisis in goal, Ian "Chico" Hamilton was brought in to play up front alongside Biggs. Chico, aged 23, had come through the Rovers ranks and understood the club – and had also come through a personal tragedy 18 months earlier when his brother – who was also on Rovers books – was killed in a bungalow fire.

Tann's decision to go with people whose loyalty would not be in doubt brought its rewards. Chico headed two goals, and Rovers clung on to a tense 3-2 victory to earn another chance in Division Three. It earned Hamilton two more years as the first choice partner to Biggs as Tann slowly rebuilt his team with the aim of getting out of Division Three through the top rather than the trapdoor!

Hall, another local lad who I think came from Fishponds somewhere, was also rewarded with an extended run as first choice keeper – although if I'm honest he wasn't the best. He wasn't very tall, and while he was a very brave goalkeeper as far as diving at people's feet was concerned he wasn't the most reliable at coming out for crosses. He was still a likeable character though – and a good cricketer too. But he then fell victim to the jinx that seems often to have hit Rovers goalkeepers. You'll remember the tragic tale of Bert Hoyle's car crash. Hall suffered a tragedy on the field, in a New Year's Eve match with Middlesbrough in 1966. In front of the Tote End he produced another of those brave dives – and was knocked out cold in a collision with one of Boro's forwards. They had to rush him to Frenchay hospital, where he was unconscious for days because the impact had created a blood clot in his skull, and he was kept in an ice-pack bed as the doctors fought to save his life. Happily they succeeded, but Bernard never played football again and I don't think he played cricket either. What a terrible thing for a young man who could have had such a great future.

Again, Tann's belief in the club producing it's own players was proved as 19-year-old Laurie Taylor was thrown into the side and despite his lack of experience he kept the job for the next couple of years.

It was also in 1962 that I had my own health scare – a massive heart attack as I was playing tennis in the summer. It was a Wednesday night, and I had been decorating all day stretching up a ladder to hang wallpaper in the hall and stairway of our three-storey house in Church Road. In the evening I met up with John Biggood, Geoff Bradford and Mike Coombes for a game of tennis at the Civil Service club, and we were all full of smiles and jokes. I'd had the warning signs of pins and needles during the day, but had thought nothing of it.

Well I'd just served three aces and was full of myself, and then suddenly as I went to try to hit the next one I went down like a ton of bricks with a crippling pain searing across my chest. And I don't remember anything else until I woke up in the intensive care unit of Southmead hospital with a pretty Malaysian nurse sat over me and the TV monitor screens bleeping alongside. My poor Mum, meanwhile, had been sat in the car watching the cricket on the other side of the Civil Service club and didn't even know I was ill!

I was in hospital for five weeks, and it was another seven months before I could go back to work. Every day I had to go out walking to stretch myself a little further as I rebuilt my strength, and then forever more I've had to think twice before lifting heavy weights. It's amazing to think the job I did, shifting all those big basketwork hampers and metal skips around for so many years. I shouldn't have done it, and in fact many times the players and physios like Roy Dolling and Wayne Jones helped me out by doing the lifting for me.

I still have to go back to Southmead Hospital every six months for a check-up, and they made me a member of the National Heart Survey which studies people who have suffered coronaries to look for the causes and patterns which prevent them happening again.

The experience certainly changed my life and changed me as a person. I had been smoking 40-a-day but gave up there and then, but to this day I've no idea what caused it. The surgeon's advice was that I shouldn't play badminton, squash or tennis but instead should take up swimming, walking and golf. I've done plenty of the first two, but shied away from the golf course because I know if I ever started I'd be hooked and become a terrible bore about it!

The surgeon also told me that if I ever lost my temper I would be in danger again, and that's actually served me well. I've always been able to keep reasonably calm even with all the exciting ups and downs of our club from promotion campaigns to Wembley visits. And if I've ever thought I might snap at anybody in football, be it manager, player or director, I've simply walked away and stayed calm. Maybe that's why I've made so many friends!

FRED FORD

O VER 17 years Bert became a legend at Bristol Rovers – and it took a tragedy to bring his time as manager to a premature end.

As I said earlier it was Ron Moules, together with his lovely wife Jan, who introduced me to working for the football club. And it's worth at this point giving you some idea of just how huge a role he played in Rovers' history.

As assistant secretary Ron was a perfect sidekick to John Gummow during the days in the 1950s when the club was being rebuilt. For both of them it was a seven days a week working existence, and they poured heart and soul into the demands of keeping the club going.

After a few years, however, I think that pressure simply became too much for John. He was a single man, and when his mother passed away he began to find the strain of so much responsibility building even more. Eventually he decided to go out of football, and went to work for Harveys the wine merchant instead where his organisational abilities were just as valuable but perhaps the pressure was a little less intense.

So Ron was promoted to secretary, and his painstaking brilliance began to dominate everything. While Bert dominated events on the field, Ron provided the same sort of inspiration off it. Nearly all the developments in the stadium happened during Ron's time in charge, and there was so much progress and so many fresh ideas that emerged in every area of the club.

He launched the True Blue club, a social club that was started up in rivalry to the Eastville Club. He also began to promote lotteries, and organised a market on Sundays on the Eastville car park.

The car park itself was adapted, so that a cinder football pitch emerged at the back of the North Stand for use in the week for training, but still to park cars on a match day. The rapid increase in car ownership, of course, was making match day parking a major priority to be resolved. And then there was the very significant purchase of a plot of land at Hambrook which was to be converted into a training ground.

The area began as a base for the youth team games – Ron organised not only the team but a league for them to play in – and then gradually the first team began to move out there to train on several days a week.

It was a far-sighted idea in an age long before the modern era when every club expects to have its own training HQ. But then Ron was full of ideas way before his time – and not least of them was the creation of Bristol Rovers' presidents club in the mid-1950s with the help of John Goodchild, Graham Holmes, Graham Hole and Roy Cowell.

It started in the old South Stand, where Ron had the idea to try to create a special area with a few more comforts to get a bit more money out of some of the club's wealthier supporters. When the North Stand was built in the summer of 1958, the big glass area which had been designed principally for dog racing gave a perfect home for this new group to move to. Now this was long before the idea of executive boxes had formed, but Ron saw the potential of an exclusive area. And so with the help of founder members like John Goodchild and Graham Holmes, the Presidents Club was formed. Two millionaire builders – called Alec Large and Doug Lennard – who had made their money by building houses in Downend and Bradley Stoke, were also among the prime movers in a club which still raises a vast amount of money today.

Ron also resolved problems over selling tickets for big cup matches by creating outlets at Lewis's department store in Bristol city centre, and at other stores in Kingswood and Hanham. It was quite a major job to go round them all collecting in the money and handing out more tickets for sale.

As if that wasn't enough he was heavily involved in the local Football Associations, sitting on the committees both in Gloucestershire and Somerset. He was always on his way up to London for some meeting or another with people like Chris Wilcox who was the Gloucestershire FA bigwig at that time, and became the FA's vice chairman for many years.

But then whatever Ron got involved in, he was one of those people who always ended up doing it to the very best he could – and probably organising everybody else too. He qualified as a tennis umpire, and reached a high enough standard to officiate at the Redland tournament which ran every year as a warm-up to Wimbledon with all the big names like Lew Hoad, Ilie Nastase and Maria Bueno. He recruited Bert Williams to be the physio for them all during the week of the tournament, and as his friend it gave me the chance to meet many of the top players of that day.

Ron's love of tennis filtered down to the players, and he organised for them to have membership of the Civil Service club in Filton Avenue, where they often held tournaments among themselves. Peter Hooper, a blond, aggressive left winger with one of the sweetest left foots I've seen, was also a superb tennis player and reached county standard along with Geoff Bradford. And in no time it seemed Ron was vice captain of the Civil Service club, and we played together in the League for them on Friday nights during the summer. Geoff, incidentally, might have been an entertaining footballer but he was the most boring tennis player in history – he just kept lobbing the ball back to you high in the air for shot after shot and waited for you to make a mistake!

As I said, I can't imagine how Ron found the time for it all. And I can't stress enough the amount of work that both he and Jan did for Bristol Rovers. So it was probably no wonder that when Ron, sadly, suffered a heart attack and died the club hit more problems.

To be honest it brings a tear to my eye to think now of the day he died. He had been out on Friday night with the chairman to play golf at Lansdown, and they had a meal afterwards. When he got home he felt pins and needles down his arm, but tried to put it out of his mind. The following day I had to go in early, as usual, to take a school party around the ground, and Ron asked me to sit down and talk to him. He said: "I've got something to tell you. I've had a funny turn, and I've been to see the doctor. He's diagnosed it as a migraine, but it was peculiar because earlier this morning I couldn't feel one side of my body and I had pins and needles. I've got to take some tablets, so will you go to Boots the Chemist tonight and get them for me."

Ron, Jan and I always used to go to a restaurant called the 49 Steps at the bottom of Christmas Steps in the City Centre for a meal on a Saturday after a game, and so we agreed I'd get the tablets on the way there. Jan knew nothing about it – she was out selling programmes and helping as she always did. Ron stayed sat down all afternoon, and I knew something was wrong. But after the game the doctor told him he was okay, reminded him to collect the tablets, and we set off into town. He was driving, and at Bond Street took a wrong turn and ended up going along the wrong side of the road. Jan asked him what the matter was. What was he doing? But Ron didn't even realise his mistake until we got to the roundabout at the other end of the road. He dropped me by Boots in the city centre to get the tablets, and I walked back down to meet them at the 49 Steps where we ate our meal. From there we went back to Eastville and the True Blue club, where we enjoyed a few more drinks.

Daft as it may seem I had to leave early. However old I was then my Mum still insisted I didn't stay out too late! So when I left the club at midnight, Ron was on his feet singing an Al Jolson number and everything seemed fine.

Sadly it wasn't. A police car came to my house shortly afterwards and they asked if I would go to Frenchay hospital, where Ron had been taken after collapsing. I went there and found him laying on a bed of ice, with the biggest bung you have ever seen in his mouth where they were trying to help him breathe. He was like that until he passed away at four o'clock on Sunday afternoon, and it was one of the saddest days of my life. He had been an incredible friend to me, and helped shape my entire life with Bristol Rovers. But however massive it was as a personal loss, the impact on the club was even more massive.

Ron had been good at delegating, with Pete Terry as assistant secretary and a lady called Marje Hall to help too. But he was the man who made everything tick, and without him the fabric of the club was going to face problems.

So it was decided that Bert Tann should move up to become general manager-secretary, and Fred Ford was invited to rejoin the club as team boss.

You'll remember that Fred had been a vital partner to Bert as his coach back in the early, progressive days of the 1950s. So it might sound a natural step for them to work together again. That, however, was far from the case because their relationship had been put through a few trials and tribulations in the intervening years.

The trouble blew up in the summer of 1960 for the simplest of reasons. Ford, whose reputation as the coach behind Tann's management was growing, was invited to become manager at Bristol City for twice the amount of money he was already earning. The first I knew of it was one Sunday night. Together with Ron and Jan I had been away on a short break to Westward Ho, and as we returned we found Fred sitting on the doorstep of their home. He broke the news to us that he'd been offered the job at Ashton Gate and had decided to take it.

It wasn't only the money that influenced him. He had worked at Carlisle alongside the great Bill Shankly, and had been in touch with the legendary Liverpool manager to ask his advice. Shanks had chided him that he was too scared to go out on his own, and told him he should go off and prove his own ability. So he'd decided that was what he must do.

When Bert got to hear of it he was furious. They had been a remarkable pair working together – just as Brian Clough and Peter Taylor were in later years. And the fall-out from Tann was every bit as bitter as happened between Clough and Taylor in their time. The two of them didn't speak for ages, and it was a long, slow process rebuilding their friendship. The fact that Ford took some of the staff over with him hardly helped. He got Jim Crawford to join him as youth team coach, and even poached a local schoolteacher called Bert Francis to help his cause. Fred wasn't worried. He was looking after number one.

Oddly enough it took Rovers being relegated for the rift to heal. That meant Ford had to bring his Bristol City team to Eastville for the first time and the two of them took the chance to talk like men and resolve their differences.

I can just imagine Fred's firm handshake as he and Bert agreed to bury the hatchet. You see Fred had lost the index finger on his right hand during the war, and when he shook hands he used to jab the little stump into the palm of your hand. It would send a sort of jarring sensation right up through your funny bone into the whole of your body, and it was a sort of a test of whether you were man enough to know him.

Bert passed the test, and by the time Fred won promotion with Bristol City in 1965, even though Rovers remained stuck in Division Three, their row had passed. City, however, were less than happy with Ford's record once they got into the Second Division, and in 1967 they sacked him. So he went off to Swindon to work as coach, and it was from there that Rovers recalled him to Eastville.

Ford's great strength had always been in finding young talent, and he set about bringing in some promising kids to change the team. The first priority was to find a centre-forward because the great Alfie Biggs had played the last of his 424 games for Rovers just before Fred took over. And he also wanted a partner for Stuart Taylor in the centre of defence.

Taylor, who began life as a plumber while playing as an amateur for Bristol City, was just 20 but at 6ft 5ins tall and 14st 6lbs in weight was a massive traditional centre-half. In theory you should have found an experienced partner to go with him, but Fred's faith in youth was such that he went instead for a 19-year-old by the name of Larry Lloyd.

Larry was Marje Hall's brother, and having been given his debut at the start of the 1968-9 season he never missed a game until the following April when Liverpool paid £55,000 to take him off to Anfield for what was then a Rovers club record for an outgoing transfer fee.

Lloyd and Taylor were a perfect partnership that season, and the rumours had gone around for ages that Liverpool were watching them. Everybody believed it would be Taylor who was sold – but in the event Lloyd went on to star in First Division and European competition both for Liverpool and Nottingham Forest while Stuart stayed where he was to rattle up an astonishing 546 League appearances for Rovers – still a record to this day.

At centre-forward he brought through another youngster from the club's developing nursery in South Wales – a boy called Wayne Jones. Wayne was an excellent header of the ball, brave and fearless, and Fred spotted the potential converting him from midfield to a striker.

There were times when Fred seemed to be making progress with his youngsters. The club went on a wonderful FA Cup run and reached the quarter-finals, losing by just one goal to Everton at Goodison Park in front of 55,294 people. I remember that game was postponed the first time it was due to be played because of snow. I had driven right up to Church Strettton near Ludlow in a Mini before I heard the news the game was off and had to turn round and go all the way back home again!

Ford was superb at organising all the training, getting the lads sorted out in Eastville Park one day and Hambrook another. He had a meticulous way of working, always keeping a careful check on who was injured and why. I recall he organised a circuit run around the stadium at Eastville for training on one day a week, and some of the players tried to dodge the hard work by hiding in a telephone box halfway round, throwing a bucket of water over each other so they appeared to have been sweating, and then running round as if they had done the whole lap. It didn't take Fred long to spot those tricks, and anybody he caught cheating ended up doing the whole thing a few extra times for luck!

I don't know whether Fred was forced to sell Larry Lloyd, or if he was unhappy about the way the club was developing. But after just one full season he was on the move again – this time returning to Swindon to become their manager.

He stayed in football and ultimately worked for many years at Oxford, where his ability to spot young talent never changed. He found many of the players who took Oxford into the First Division in the 1980s. The last time I saw him was at Eastville when he came with Oxford's reserve team.

You'll remember he was a tall man, well able to take the mickey out of himself, and I started to laugh at him because his suit was miles too big for him because of the weight he had lost. When he then told me quietly that he wouldn't be here for much longer I wasn't sure how to take it. Sadly he was all too serious, and he died of cancer in October 1981 within a few days of the death of his great friend Bill Shankly. The church at Whitchurch where his funeral was held was packed with people from all over the world of football. There were people from the FA, from clubs, officials from the Football League, former players, and also the press and TV and radio. That was the respect in which he was held.

BILL DODGIN

BERT Tann's influence as general manager must have been vital in keeping the ship steady as Fred walked out after barely more than a year in charge. It was a case of turning to the people he knew and trusted.

And there couldn't have been anybody at the club who better fitted that description than Bill Dodgin, who was named first caretaker manager and then put in permanent charge.

Bill was a man who had been there and done that at every level of football, having played before the war for Huddersfield, Lincoln and significantly Charlton where he had become firm friends with Tann.

He then managed Southampton, and moved on to Fulham where his achievements included the discovery of the great Johnny Haynes. He had also rounded off his football education by spending time as coach to Sampdoria in Italy – at that time a unique idea for an Englishman to work abroad. When he came back to England Bert persuaded him to move down to Bristol to become Chief Scout and the eye for talent which had found Haynes began to go to work again.

Bill had played a key role in helping Ford's efforts to bring in new young talent, and because he had both played and more importantly managed at the highest levels he had contacts throughout the game.

He used them to bring in his first key signing, a giant of a goalkeeper from West Bromwich Albion called Dick Shepherd. Bill got him on a free transfer, and it proved a superb piece of talent spotting. Dick was 6ft 2ins and built with a massive frame, and was also a lively, bubbly character of a person – one of those people you could sit and talk to for hours on end. Bill felt he wanted a bigger, more dominant goalkeeper and that meant the end of the road fairly quickly for Laurie Taylor who was only 22 but found himself out of the first team reckoning and he ended up going into part-time football with Chelmsford in Essex.

Bill also found a young right winger by the name of Ray Graydon to give some balance to an attack where long-serving Harold Jarman was a fixture on the left wing. He also brought in a centre-forward from Torquay called Robin Stubbs who in the summer months worked as a deckchair attendant on the front in the seaside town – and used to tell you he earned more out of deckchairs than football.

Bill's first season was a superb success, adding Tony Ford as a new signing from Bristol City at full-back and then bringing in blond-haired Carl Gilbert to play up front instead of Bobby Jones. Gilbert, who had bought himself out of the army to start playing professional football at Gillingham, began to get goals and by March, Dodgin looked likely to clinch promotion back to Division Two. As deadline day loomed he took the decision to strengthen the side by bringing in Don Megson as an experienced player-coach. In theory the arrival of a man who captained Sheffield Wednesday's FA Cup winners a few years earlier ought to have been the signing that clinched a place in the top two. In practice it didn't work out like that and although Megson's debut was a 1-0 win over Orient, they managed only one more victory from the final six games and finished third.

His second season started with a severe blow when Ford was accidentally kicked in his back during a game by Dick Sheppard, and was left with a problem with his spleen. Tony to this day has to take medication because of it. Tony had played for the Ashton Gate club for eight years before joining Rovers – but despite that I suspect his heart is in blue and white quarters rather than red now because he still often comes to games.

Bill reshaped the side with Phil Roberts taking over at right-back at the same time as long-serving Alex Munro's days were ended and

Lindsay Parsons became the regular left-back. He also brought in another young Welshman called Frankie Prince to win the ball in midfield.

Rovers side was beginning to get quite an influence from South Wales. The newly-built Severn Bridge had suddenly opened up that area as a nursery for young talent because it was easily accessible. And Bill Dodgin did more than most to exploit that opportunity, putting Stan Montgomery in charge of a series of nurseries for talented schoolboy footballers. Stan had been a magnificent centre-half for Cardiff in their First Division days just after the war, and was as good at spotting a young player as he had once been at spotting a dangerous attack. He was also a county cricketer for Essex for many years, and we'd spend many an hour on reserve team coach journeys listening to him telling tales from the cricket circuit, or arguing about who was the best batsman or bowler at any given time.

About this time I was given the honour of travelling away with the team for the first time, providing it was on days when there was no reserve game at home and I wasn't needed on the microphone.

It began for not the best of reasons. John Hare, one of the directors who was also on the stadium company board, suffered a partial stroke and when he was well enough to go to football again he needed a chaperone. It was quite a chore – especially as it included having to help him go to the toilet.

John liked a drop of scotch – and then another drop and a drop more! I recall one game at Fulham where we had been entertained in the office of their manager Bobby Campbell (no relation to our own Bobby Campbell), along with their very colourful chairman Ernie Clay. They gave John a bottle of scotch, and I took him out on to the balcony of the Cottage with the biggest jug of water you ever saw. He set about drinking the lot – and I had to take him to the toilet more than once in the first half and it seemed every five minutes in the second! It was a rotten job – but I didn't mind because it was just something else that brought me into the fold at the football club I loved.

Bill's side hit a sensational run in which they lost only three of 30 matches in all competitions between the beginning of September and 2

January. And one of those defeats was in a League Cup quarter final replay at Aston Villa and happened only after a thrilling 1-1 draw at Eastville.

That Cup run was to shape things for Rovers again, because Graydon played superbly in both matches and Villa became determined to sign him. They ultimately agreed to pay £25,000 and add in Welsh captain Brian Godfrey as a part exchange deal. Graydon went on to score 68 goals in 188 games for Villa, was popular there and is now highly successful as a manager at Walsall.

Critically Don Megson, who was so important alongside giant Stuart Taylor at the back during that run in the first half of the season, began to suffer injury problems and without him the momentum was lost. Bill's team finished sixth and were again left only to wonder what might have been.

The swop in the summer of Graydon for Godfrey helped fill the gap left because Megson decided it was time to hang up his boots and step down from playing just to concentrate on coaching. And Godfrey was a tower of strength. He gave the team some backbone and it wasn't long before he was made captain. He was a Welshman and proud of it, and coming from Villa he wanted the same sort of big club standards at Eastville.

Bill's teams needed good defenders, because he took huge risks with his style of play. Bill loved attacking football. He wanted to entertain the public, and that was what he set out to do. He was also a nice man who looked after the younger players – although he could have his faults too.

There was a promising young player called Dave Pugsley who used to go training twice a week out on the ashes on the back of the North Stand, and one night got in a collision with Jackie Pitt who put him down on the floor and damaged his knee. For the next 15 months Dave had to go twice a week for treatment while he was studying at college, and was doing his best to get back to fitness. Unfortunately one day when the other players had come in from training, and found Dave still having treatment, Bill was in mischievous mood and started taking the mickey, telling him: "There's nothing wrong with your knee, it's all in the mind." Poor Dave was so frustrated by the amount of time and effort he'd spent, to no avail, trying to get fit that he lost his temper and got off the bed and laid Bill out with one punch. Dave waited for him to come round, and told the manager: "I didn't hit you. You only thought I did. It was all in your mind!"

I think Bill regretted what he'd said, but needless to say Dave got the sack later that day. Bert as general manager wouldn't entertain the idea of blows between members of staff, and certainly not against the team manager. Dodgin's great belief, as I said, was in finding young talent and bringing the discoveries through. The Welsh nursery began to thrive, and they also recruited a young supporter called Gordon Bennett to help Montgomery, a former Cardiff City player, with all the administration.

Gordon was a bit of an oddball character who used to stand on the terracing in the front of the South Enclosure and blow a french horn. The noise annoyed the directors so much that they began to wonder how they could silence him – and Bert Tann said there was only one way to beat him – give him a job! So they appointed him on the youth development side and his enthusiasm and attention to detail became vital in helping find all the promising players from Wales who contributed to much to Rovers' next ten years. Just to show his enthusiasm for the club Gordon went on an amazing sponsored walk around all 92 clubs in the League which brought much needed money into the club.

Dodgin enjoyed another good League Cup run in his third season – reaching the quarter-finals – but again the team could finish no higher than sixth despite putting together a five-match winning run in the League. His biggest problem was always finding a reliable goalscorer, and he ultimately gave up the hope of bringing through his own talent and went to Bradford to spend a club record £23,000 in November 1971 on Bruce Bannister. As often happens with a new, big-money centre-forward, however, Bruce took some time to settle in but with 15goals from 32 League and Cup games in his first season looked as if he would be a successful investment. In the summer Bill was moved sideways to return to his role as chief scout, and the young, track-suited Don Megson was given the chance to take control.

DON MEGSON

B Y this time I was more and more involved in the club, working as a volunteer it seemed on most nights of the week. I was chairman of the True Blue club, being run by Ted Osbourne, and got to know all the players and people behind the scenes. I was also chairman of the lottery, and spent Monday nights touring out around Yate on a motorcycle with my 70-year-old Mum riding pillion as we went collecting up the money from the various agents who sold lottery tickets before bringing it back to count. That was Monday, and then it was much the same routine around other places for every other night.

My Dad had died in May 1960 at the age of just 64, and as my brother and sisters had all moved away it meant I had to take on the job of looking after Mum. It would be wrong to say I was lumbered with the task because like anybody I loved my Mum and was happy to take care of her. She would come out with me on my lottery rounds, and used to enjoy going to occasional Rovers games. Then on Sundays I would always take her out for the day in the Austin Mini I proudly drove – we'd head down to Somerset or Devon for the coast. But it did mean that between all the work I did for Rovers, and looking after my Mum, I didn't have much time for any other form of enjoyment.

There were all sorts of extra jobs at Rovers too as the club found every last way to save money. Before midweek reserve games it was my job together with Derek Reece, the electrician, to put the floodlights on. There was a sequence of switches to follow – tower number one first because it contained a booster circuit, then three, then two, then four. I was warned several times to concentrate on getting the right order because if you didn't it would blow the fuses and leave the match in darkness – as well as costing more money for repairs! There was also a strict instruction on reserve nights that the lights must not go on before 7pm when the cheap rate electricity started. The players couldn't go out to warm up, but at least the club saved a few bob!

Thankfully one job I didn't have was cleaning the lights. The soot and grit from the gasworks meant that had to be done once every six weeks, and I think if they had ever asked me to scale the 146 ft high tower it would have been the only time in 51 years I ever refused to do a job to help the Rovers!

I was also still doing all the match day announcing, and it had now become a regular event when the reserves weren't at home on a Saturday – because if they were I had to be there on the microphone just the same – that I was able to travel away on the team bus.

So even though I didn't earn a penny from Rovers, I felt they were my club and I belonged to them. And when Don took charge and immediately won a trophy for the first time in the club's history I couldn't have been more ecstatic.

Megson had brought in high standards from the day he arrived. To be honest when he first came I wasn't sure I liked him. I thought he was a bit arrogant. But then if you think about his achievements with his previous club he had every right to be like that. He was a cut and a swagger above the rest because he had done it with Sheffield Wednesday. And he brought those standards with him, making his presence felt from day one as a coach.

He arrived to back up Bill Dodgin with many of the modern ideas that were spreading through the top of the game. How much he added his own ideas, and how much he simply copied those he had seen and learned at Hillsborough, I don't know. But once he was given total control of the team he was even more determined that things would be done his way.

There were little things that were typical of this new professionalism. He started making all the players wear shower shoes to protect their feet after training – pretty obvious when you think that half the players from a previous team suffered from verrucas! He also encouraged the players to drink water. Until then they had simply taken a swig and spat it out – not like modern players who seem to drink it by the gallon!

He bought a house at Frenchay near to what was rapidly becoming the club's headquarters on the training ground at Hambrook, and moved most of the practice sessions to the grass pitches there instead of the old cinder area at Eastville. So much of what he did appears just common sense now, but then it was a major innovation. The training kit, for instance, used to be left ready for the players in the morning as one big pile of shirts, another of shorts, and another of socks. Whoever got in earliest got the best gear, and if you were late every day you probably got socks full of holes! Don started getting everything numbered so that every player had their own personal training kit to take care of.

Don wasn't a big man. He was about 5ft 9ins in height, and probably didn't weigh more than 12 stone wet through, but he had been a ferocious tackler as a player and he was equally aggressive as a manager. He would shout and bawl at people and make sure he let them knew exactly what he wanted.

That was of course a big change from Bill Dodgin, who tended to nurture people along with soft words and was very laid back with people. He believed in attacking flair on the field and laughter off it. His favourite saying was: "Happy when you win, smile when you lose, and the smoke goes up the chimney just the same". Don didn't quite follow that creed – and certainly wasn't often to be found smiling when Rovers lost!

He got off to the perfect start, however, by winning a pre-season tournament called the Watney Cup. It sounds incredible now to think it had any importance whatever, but at that time there was a move to build a tournament before the season kicked-off and give it the same sort of profile that the Football League Cup had managed to establish itself.

We beat First Division Wolves 2-0 at home in the first round, then went to Turf Moor and won by the same scoreline against Burnley – who would later that season win promotion to the First Division. And that meant a final at home to First Division Sheffield United, with nearly 20,000 turning out to see if Rovers after nearly 90 years of history could actually win a national competition.

The day didn't get off to the best of starts. In those days we used to have all sorts of pre-match entertainment, and it being a final they laid on the works. Besides having the police dogs doing a demonstration, and the Fishponds Legion band, they had the idea to bring the ball in by parachute. Good idea – except the parachutist lost his bearings and landed on the gasometer a couple of hundred yards away!!

It was a roasting hot day, as I remember, and Don inspired his team to play way above themselves. There was some exciting football played in that game, I can tell you, and United's teenage goalkeeper Tom McAlister was in inspired form to keep the final scoreline at 0-0.

So it went to penalties, and I can recall the mounting excitement as before each one I had to announce what was going on. "Taking penalty number three for Rovers is Bruce Bannister," and so on. Eventually Dick Sheppard saved the 14th kick of a nail biting competition, and Rovers had won 7-6. I'd like to say I stayed professional and simply announced the score, but I'm not sure I did! I was very emotional, and the excitement when the Cup was presented on the pitch was fantastic.

We believed that was setting the scene for the promotion season that everybody wanted, and another run in the League Cup seemed to back that up. John Rudge, who had joined us from Torquay the previous year in a swop deal for Robin Stubbs, appeared to be a promising centre-forward alongside Bannister and they got a goal each in a fantastic League Cup win against Manchester United at Old Trafford which took us into the fourth round.

Don had given the whole place an air of importance, taking his players to a pre-match meal at the Crest hotel to give them a taste of how things were done at the top. And he also was keen to push them out into the community to both promote the club and get a feel of their own importance to the people who supported them.

He was also very keen on giving the young apprentices a feeling of how lucky they were and some idea of what the outside world might be like if they didn't make it. He felt they should have an education, and he instigated a scheme where once a month they would visit a different factory – perhaps at Cadbury's to see the chocolate being made, or at Willis where I worked producing cigarettes, or down on the docks where Bristol's identity as a port city was still intact.

The old "no-buy, no-sell" days had been consigned to the history books, and Megson pushed the directors to find more money to be ambitious and bring in other players. He needed to, as well, because he had awful luck with two key injuries that first season. Shepherd, the outstanding goalkeeper who incidentally saved a penalty from George Best to earn that replay at Old Trafford, fractured his skull diving at the feet of Tranmere forward Eddie Loyden. And also Wayne Jones, such a bubbly, funny character as well as being a forward of great promise, had to give up the game because of a knee injury that was diagnosed as a rare bone condition.

Megson went across the bridge to Cardiff to solve the goalkeeping problem, somehow picking up the 6ft 4ins Scotsman Jim Eadie on a free transfer. He was a huge man with a great big barrel chest, who was always overweight and loved both his food and his drink – and how hard they had to push him in training to keep him fit enough to play I don't know! Push him they certainly did, however, and Jim played 200 games over the next few years and was a vital influence in the success which Megson was to enjoy.

He also managed to get Colin Dobson, who had played with him at Hillsborough, on a free transfer. He was a magnificently skilfull outside-left who could cross the ball with either foot, and was a cut above anything else in our division at that time. I would often watch him and wonder what he was doing at that level because he was so much more classy than anything else. He was also a forthright talker who had strong views on the game, and he ended up getting involved in a lot of the coaching.

That was typical of how Megson had changed the atmosphere. Once he became manager he altered as a person, and made it clear he was no longer one of the players. He put some distance between himself and the rest of the dressing-room, and if he wanted something done he didn't stand for any arguing. I may have had my suspicions at first but I grew to like Don, but then I wasn't a player and I'm not sure he was entirely popular with them!

He certainly fell out with Brian Godfrey, who for all his skill and passing quality didn't have the aggressive edge that Megson wanted. The Welsh captain was moved gently back across the bridge to Newport at the end of his first season. That meant more opportunity for a younger Welshman called Frankie Prince who may not have been as skilful but would kick seven bells out of anybody to win the ball! There was no finesse about Frankie, but Don didn't want any either. His job was to win the ball and give it to the others to roll it about.

The most crucial signing, however, came in March when Don smashed the transfer record yet again to bring in another old Hillsborough team mate called Alan Warboys. Immediately Rovers had found the right partner for Bruce Bannister, and the partnership known as "Smash and Grab" was born.

I think in football that every team always seeks two strikers who fit together. And I think that the best double acts like that just happen instinctively. The moment the two of them first team up you know it will work.

Bannister and Warboys were just like that. Bruce was small and sharp, while Warboys was six feet tall and strong, and together they shared 15 goals in the last ten games of the season. It was too late to bring a finish any higher than fifth, but the signs were all there for the year to follow.

Megson's team began the next season like a runaway train, winning seven of their first nine games and staying unbeaten in the

League in 27 matches, right up until the start of February. The crowds who had been mainly coming to the big Cup ties were now starting to roll up in the League as well, with 22,000 packed into Eastville for a Boxing Day 4-2 win over Plymouth.

And of course there was that magical day at the Goldstone Ground when Bannister got three and Warboys four in an amazing 8-2 thrashing of Brighton. I was lucky because there was no reserve game that weekend, and so I joined the team which went and stayed overnight on the Friday evening.

All the talk was of how Brighton, with the great Brian Clough and Peter Taylor having just taken over, were about to do great things. The TV cameras from *Match of the Day* had even been sent to record what was expected to be the start of the progress of football's most famous and controversial double act. But we had a relaxing Friday night and on the day simply every shot we had flew in. Some games just go like that.

Clough and Taylor were furious, and I think completely changed the team around after that, getting rid of many of the players who had been beaten. For us it simply confirmed that Megson's side were on a roll, and we followed it with another Warboys hat-trick in a 4-0 win over Southend at home a week later.

The only place we didn't have success that year was in the Cups – although we did make a little bit of history by figuring in one of the first matches played on a Sunday. That was a 4-3 defeat at Nottingham Forest in the FA Cup's third round in January, when Ted Heath's three-day week and power restrictions saw games being moved back so they didn't need floodlights.

Like most good teams it was built on a solid defence, with Trevor Jacobs and Lindsay Parsons the two full-backs and skipper Mike Green, Don's first signing after taking over a year earlier, as solid as a rock alongside the giant Stuart Taylor.

But it was always going to be Smash and Grab who were the stars. They were the men who got the goals, and the headlines, after all.

"Smash" was Warboys, a warm friendly Yorkshireman who was a good family man. He was very popular with the other players – in fact I'd say they almost idolised him because he was getting the goals for them. He liked a bet, mind. He would bet on two flies going up a wall if he had the chance but then a few of them were like that and it simply added to the team spirit. They organised little competitions among themselves at the Eastville club at billiards, table tennis or snooker – always for money – and even some of the former players used to come back and join in. Yet however competitive Alan might have been in all those competitions, he was a big gentle man and I don't think I ever saw him lose his temper. He was always calm, always controlled and everybody liked him.

"Grab", his mate Bannister, was a livewire little man who was a man of the world. Whether he had actually done all the things he bragged about I don't know, but he was always telling some story of what he had done in life. He was only a short fellow, at about 5ft 9ins, but he was very brave and like any good goalscorer wasn't afraid to go in where it hurt. I saw him score goals where he dived across a centre-half's foot and headed the ball from two or three feet off the ground just before the hapless defender thought he was going to kick it away.

Bruce loved the adulation of the crowd, he liked to get them all going and they would play up to him. He'd argue with referees if he thought he was in the right. In fact he'd argue with anybody if he thought he was in the right! He had a sharp brain and was involved on the Players' Union committee which helped negotiate the end of the old retain and transfer system.

That brainpower served him well when he stopped playing because he has been exceptionally successful in business. He runs a huge sports business, and has a massive building which is almost like an aircraft hanger back in his home town of Bradford, from where he deals in boats and jetski bikes as well as football boots and trainers. The last time I met him was when Rovers played at Bradford and Bruce had an executive box there. I'd been there early to set the kit out, and he came down to find me and invited me up to join him for a drink. He almost threw me in the air he was so pleased to see me again. That was typical of him that he thought about other people and always wanted to include you in anything that was going on.

There was a tricky period in the middle of that season when Warboys had a hamstring injury, and neither John Rudge nor Dave Staniforth who cost £20,000 just before deadline day could quite produce the same fireworks in front of goal. But despite losing 2-1 at home to eventual champions Oldham on Easter Saturday, the team clung on to second place and eventually clinched a return to Division Two with a 0-0 draw at Southend. Around 1,000 fans travelled right across the country to see it. Southend by road was always one of the longest journey times, so everybody went by train to be sure they didn't get there late.

The celebrations that followed were wonderful. Nearly 20,000 watched the last game of the season – ironically against a much improved Brian Clough's Brighton team who forced a 1-1 draw. But my memories are of the civic day when the whole club were invited to the Council House on College Green in Bristol. We sat down to lunch with a succession of speeches toasting the football club, toasting the city of Bristol, toasting everybody. Those are the happy times in football and you have to enjoy it. The team went out on the balcony to salute their fans, with a giant crowd of blue and white cheering from below. It was very emotional, and we believed great things were on their way.

Life is never that simple though, is it? Smash and Grab might have terrorised the Third Division, but at a level higher people knew about them and set out to stop them. And the partnership which produced 40 goals between them in the promotion season returned 20 then 16 then 15 in the next three years.

You only have to look at the clubs who were in Division Two in 1974-75 to realise what a tough division it was. Manchester United had been relegated and were storming back to the top flight under Tommy Docherty. In competition too were Sunderland, Sheffield Wednesday, Aston Villa, and Southampton – all big clubs who belonged at a higher level. And Fulham were in the middle of a romantic spell of ambition under Alec Stock, when they signed England's World Cup-winning captain Bobby Moore, re-signed Alan Mullery from Spurs, and later on persuaded George Best to join them.

I actually hitched a lift on Fulham's team bus back to London after the game to have a night out in town. By this time I'd been around the game enough to start to have friends and felt confident – as well as a bit cheeky – to make the request to any of the London teams who came to Eastville. I remember being impressed as every Fulham player who got back on their bus was handed a metal box about 15 inches square. When you opened it there were two layers – the first with a pineapple already neatly cut up, a banana and an apple, and then in the lower section was a piece of chicken and a cold pork steak with some dry biscuits to go with it. That was their after-match meal, intended to be more healthy than the fish and chips that many clubs provided – and still do to this day.

Mind you, it was ironic that Fulham should be so concerned about nutrition when I tell you about George Best's antics when he played for them at Eastville in February 1977.

I happened to have needed to leave my microphone for a few minutes before the game to take a message up to the dressing-rooms. I was making my way back so that I could announce the teams, when I realised that the Rovers players had already gone out from the lower dressing-room while Fulham were leaving theirs higher up the tunnel. I waited for the players to go ahead of me and Best was last to come out.

Now halfway down the corridor was a telephone box, where Fulham's coach driver was standing out of the way. As Best came past he took a plastic bottle from the coach driver containing about a third of a pint of liquid, drank it all down in one go, and threw the bottle to one side. The drink, and Bestie, disappeared as quick as a flash, and I assumed it must be some sort of health drink. Out of interest I picked the bottle up and smelt what was left of its contents – and realised it was neat Pernod! I asked the coach driver what Best was doing, and he simply shrugged and said: "Oh he always has that before a game."

During these few years I was lucky enough to meet many other great footballing people who came to Eastville. I had acquired another job serving drinks in the boardroom after matches – which

I still do now – and it gave me the opportunity to make many friends. Tommy Docherty sticks out as a man who was always forthright in his views, called a spade a spade, and was always willing to give you time to talk to you.

Among the younger players Don Megson was bringing through was his son Gary, who by the way gets his distinctive ginger hair from his lovely mum. I remember Gary getting upset with me after he had made his reserve team debut in a match at Eastville. It was a late change to the printed team, so as announcer I had called out: "Coming in at number six is the manager's son, Gary Megson". Gary, with dad in attendance, confronted me afterwards and said: "What was all that about, announcing me as 'the manager's son?'" I suppose like many young players with influential fathers he wanted to be recognised in his own right. I was a bit taken a back, but said: "Well you aren't his f******g daughter, are you?" It left them both speechless.

One of the more professional things Don introduced were end of season tours to exotic places. First they went to Australia, New Zealand and Bangkok. And then later there was another trip to America. And it was there that I think Don was entranced by the flair and razzamatazz with which the pioneers of soccer in the States were trying to sell the game. I think he may have been tapped up about joining the revolution while he was there. Certainly he and secretary Pete Terry both enjoyed a terrific social time on the tour and were very influenced by everything they saw.

He had also been forced to sell Bannister and then Warboys, and was turning more and more to the products of the club's Welsh nursery to take the team forward. He brought an 18-year-old Martin Thomas in to play in goal instead of Jim Eadie and encouraged other Welsh boys like Peter Aitken, Phil Bater, David Williams and Andrew Evans. Evans was a highly-talented striker, and it was tragic that he suffered a terrible broken leg in a match against Southampton at Eastville right in front of the North Stand. He was in hospital for ages, and never played again. And incidentally Lawrie McMenemy, Southampton's renowned manager, never once got in touch to ask how he was, which rather disappointed us because I thought he was a nicer man.

Megson paid £10,000 to Wolves for the experienced Bobby Gould to try to add some strength up front, and it looked a good move when he got a hat-trick on his debut in a 4-1 win over Blackburn. But the very next game we suffered an amazing 9-0 defeat against Tottenham at White Hart Lane that killed the confidence all over again. Goalkeeper Thomas missed that trip because of an injury, and a young lad called Glyn Jones – yet another from the Welsh nursery – was in goal. Poor Glyn got reminded of that day forever. He actually ended up coaching the goalkeepers for the Welsh national side but whenever anybody sees him now they always pull his leg about his big day at White Hart Lane!

As the 1977-8 season continued to unfold Rovers had recorded just three wins in the first 19 games, and Don was growing increasingly frustrated at how he was being forced to rely on youngsters when he had once been able to pay record transfer fees. He began to feel the grass would be greener across the Atlantic, and was then given an opportunity to taste the American flair for himself with the chance to manage Portland Timbers in the North American Soccer League. In November 1977 he resigned to take his chance, and Rovers were in crisis yet again.

BOBBY CAMPBELL

L OSING a manager in mid-season is a traumatic time for any club, and all the more so for Rovers' directors at that time. Faced with a relegation fight they needed a quick decision, and so it made sense to promote Bobby Campbell from within.

At 55 years old, Bobby gave the club the same sort of experience, stability and perspective that Bill Dodgin had offered before. The two of them had arrived at Eastville almost at the same time nearly two decades earlier and knew the club inside out. Bobby had been introduced by Bert Tann as a trainer, and took the physiotherapist side of things on as well.

Bobby's playing pedigree was top rate. A skilful winger, he made his full debut for Scotland against England at outside-right with Matt Busby playing behind him at wing half, and scored in front of 120,000 people at Hampden. He talks to this day of how Busby never played a pass to him that was above a foot high, and there's no doubt that the man who went on to make Manchester United great in the 1960s had a profound influence on the young Campbell. Bobby started out playing for Falkirk, and then went to Chelsea where he supplied the crosses that the great Tommy Lawton turned into goals. After 188 games for the Stamford Bridge club he became trainer at

Reading and then briefly went back to Scotland to manage Dumbarton before Bert brought him to Bristol.

Now Bobby might have been 55 years old when he took charge of Bristol Rovers, but his enthusiasm and energy would have done justice to somebody 30 years younger. On the entrance to the field of play there appeared a large notice proclaiming: "Campbell's blue and white army". And like any good general he was thorough and conscientious, travelling to see the youth teams and reserves.

He was a stickler for discipline and good timing. If he said that training was due to start at ten o'clock then he meant ten o'clock and not a second later. If anybody was late they were fined for it – as simple as that.

Bobby lived up on Horfield Common – near to Rovers home at the Memorial Stadium today – but spent so much time either travelling to see games or working at the ground or the newly developing Hambrook training complex that really it was probably just as well he was so close to work because I guess he didn't get to spend much time at home anyway!

Bobby faced the relegation fight he was left with head-on, bringing in another product of the club's Welsh academies in the form of aggressive midfield man Tony Pulis. He also decided to show confidence in a young lad called Paul Randall who had been recruited from non-League football – and instantly found another fans folk hero.

Randall, "Punky" as we used to call him, was one of those young lads who had trailed around a series of unsuccessful trials as a kid and at the age of nearly 20 had effectively given up trying to be a footballer and had gone to work in his home town of Glastonbury. He was described as a "trainee supermarket manager", but I think that really just meant he spent his working days restocking the shelves!

He'd been noticed in Western League football with Glastonbury and Frome town, and had been invited for a trial in the summer just a few months before Megson moved on. Rovers staff were obviously impressed because they agreed to pay Frome £50,000 for him, which was a staggering amount of money to spend on a non-League player then.

He appeared in the side only a few times while Megson was in charge, but Bobby decided to throw him straight in and for the rest of that year he couldn't stop scoring goals. He finished with 20 from 28 games, and the fans loved not only his flowing black curly hair but the feeling he was one of them. Paul loved to celebrate his goals with the supporters, and the romantic story of moving from filling supermarket shelves to hitting goals was one that every dreamer in the crowd could identify with.

At the same time Bob had another of Megson's last signings – the experienced Bobby Gould – playing up front for him and the side put together an eight-match unbeaten run that hauled them away from trouble and into 18th place.

As I said, Bobby's great quality was his enthusiasm. And for an example of that I need only think of an away trip to Newcastle. I used to get time off on a Friday afternoon to travel with them, and we set off from Bristol at midday in March for the long journey to an overnight stop at Chester-le-Street in Durham, a few miles outside Newcastle.

We had a coach driver called Greg from Clevedon who would get you anywhere, but even his ability got tested as the weather closed in while we went north. There were patches of snow and thick fog, and it was the early hours of Saturday morning before we even reached Scotch Corner. The fog, ice and snow was so bad by now that we had to have somebody walking in front of the coach to guide the way. We had a lovely Irish lad called Miah Dennehy who had been offloaded from Nottingham Forest by Brian Clough, and while everybody else thought Bobby was taking the mickey in asking for volunteers to go ahead, Miah just offered to go first. In the event the lads took it in turns, with the likes of Phil Bater and Peter Aitken doing a job that was a bit like in the early days of the motor car when somebody had to walk ahead waving a red flag! The snow kept coming down by the bucket load, but somehow we completed the last 20 miles in a huge detour and reached the hotel at about five in the morning – some 17 hours after we set off. Stuart Taylor was the great hero of the day, seeming to walk miles.

Bob's instructions were to get everybody off to bed, with a warning that he'd wake us all up later. We laughed because you could just see outside that the snow was drifting feet deep in places, and the coach was already nearly buried in the few minutes since we'd arrived. But sure enough after only a few hours sleep he wanted everybody up for a training session. We all thought he was having a joke but Bob was deadly serious. He was still hoping the game would go ahead and organised everybody to do a light running session in the hotel corridors! The coach by now was completely buried, so even if there had been a miraculous heatwave a few miles down the road I still don't know how Bob thought we might get to St James's Park to play the game! In fact Bill McGarry, the Newcastle manager, didn't even bother to make contact with us at the hotel.

Saturday night was St Patrick's night, and the hotel band managed to brave it through the bad weather to perform. As I remember they were an exceptionally good group. But alas there were no ladies in the hotel to dance with so it was still a flop! We were stuck there until Monday, with people and families coming in from the motorway like refugees over the weekend and sleeping on the floors. Bob dealt with that situation too, organising more training sessions for the players to take charge of all the kids who were suddenly wandering around the hotel with nothing to do. The players were ordered to go across the fields to help the hotel management by fetching bread and milk supplies each morning.

We had to try to travel back on the Monday afternoon because we were due to play in Bristol on the Tuesday night, and it took another epic 15-hour trip. First of all we had to be transported by the police in their four wheel drive cars because the team bus just couldn't move, and so from Chester-le-Street bus station we were loaded into what seemed to be the oldest bus in the world for the journey home.

This was a momentous season for me, because it marked the moment that I stopped working for Rovers for love and began to earn money! Not much of it, mind! So maybe it still was a labour of love.

The Chancellor at the time, in his wisdom, decided to put up the duty on a packet of cigarettes by 14 pence. The move may have been welcomed by the anti-smoking lobby, but in the factory where I worked it wasn't so popular. The very next day they announced there would have to be 3,500 redundancies and my name was on the list.

Well, I got a superb pay-off to sweeten the blow. It was £30,000, which was a tremendous amount of money in those days, plus a pension. But I was still worried about where it all left me because I knew that at 50 years old I would need to earn some money.

I told Pete Terry that I was going to be out of work, and he in turn told Douglas Milne the vice chairman. In that situation you talk to everybody who might be able to offer suggestions of a new job, and I shared my worries with Graham Holmes and Graham Hole, two other directors, as well.

The next thing was that Douglas asked why didn't I come and work for Bristol Rovers? After 19 years on the lottery, and the PA announcing and chairman of the True Blue club, he felt I'd put in my service and shown my heart was in the right place! But he said I'd have to give up those duties because once I was on the staff there would be a different set of rules. You could not act as chairman of either the lottery or the True Blue club if you were employed by the parent club.

They wanted to create a new position of kit man, because Wayne Jones who after being forced to stop playing had become assistant physio and was finding it impossible to look after all the gear as well as deal with the injuries. The club had just moved its training base to Hambrook, and because the washing machines were still at Eastville it was making it quite a logistical exercise to look after all the training and playing gear.

So after all those years of clocking on at ten past seven in the morning, and working until ten past five, I suddenly had a job in football and thought I was heading for a life of riley. I soon realised it wouldn't be so simple when Douglas Milne wrote out the list of all my new duties, and before long I was working even longer hours but for seven days a week!

I loved the job, however. It meant I was involved with the players and team every day, and now always travelled with them to take care of providing teas, coffees, other drinks and food on the coach as well as looking after the matchday kit.

Away coach trips had a happy atmosphere, and while Bobby believed in showing that he was in charge he was always concerned to make sure that the spirit was good.

I remember once when we played away at Brighton, the chairman asked if his wife could travel with us, and Bob broke the normal golden rule that no women are allowed on the coach. When we got to the hotel Bobby allocated everybody their rooms, and when we went up I found I was in a huge room with a vast double bed complete with an enormous basket of fruit and a massive bunch of the most beautiful flowers you would ever see. There were two explanations – either Bobby was exceptionally pleased with the way the kit had been washed or I was in the room intended for the chairman and his lady!!

Meanwhile Stuart Taylor, our 6ft 4ins centre-half, had found himself in a tiny single room with a sloping ceiling on which he had banged his head the moment he sat up. We both went to see Bobby at about the same time to say that we were in the wrong rooms, but just got the abrupt answer in his Scottish accent: "Hell's Bells, will you not just do as I tell you?"

We played the match next day, and afterwards as I got back on the coach to start organising the food for the return journey I noticed a young lady sat on the low wall next to where we parked outside the Goldstone Ground. She was wearing a short skirt, and sitting with her legs apart displaying her wares for all the world to see.

As I made my way to the back of the coach I found that lovable rogue Miah Dennehy, who let's say had been better endowed in other parts of his body than in the common sense department, already there with his tracksuit bottoms tugged down giving the girl an eyeful of his own equipment! I shouted and bawled at him to behave but just at that moment the chairman's wife descended from the staircase at the back of the stand and could see everything before her. Suffice to say that she never travelled to an away match again!

Campbell's second season began on a sour note as he fell out with Bobby Gould. Gouldy, who had been brought to the club from Wolves only as a player but was vastly experienced having played at the top level for many clubs, wanted to have his say over how the team should play and had different opinions. He was moved on swiftly to Hereford.

Then came another bombshell when Campbell told the board he wanted to accept an offer of £170,000 from Stoke for Paul Randall. Rovers had got off to a flying start with Randall grabbing 13 goals in 21 games, and had outside promotion chances themselves. But Campbell assured the directors that it was good business because Stoke only wanted him to get promoted and if they were successful he could bring Randall back for a fraction of the money. And he also felt he had a ready-made replacement in a former England schoolboy international striker called Steve White who was emerging from the youth teams.

He was proved right on both counts. In fact White did so well he was later sold to Luton for £195,000. But the decision to sell the popular Randall backfired on Bobby because he lost the trust of the supporters who felt betrayed that their new hero had been allowed to go. And even though White picked up 10 goals in 23 games for the rest of that season, he didn't have the flair, panache and personality which made Randall so popular on the terraces.

I think Bobby was finding the pressure of the job difficult to handle. And he also had problems at home because his wife, sadly, began to suffer prematurely from Alzheimer's. So in the summer of 1979 he signed Terry Cooper from Bristol City to become his player-coach.

Now Terry was probably the most experienced player to pull on the blue and white quarters up until that time. He'd won everything in Don Revie's great Leeds team, had been recognised as arguably England's best ever left-back, and been a stalwart in the 1970 World

Cup in Mexico. And unfortunately once he started working at Rovers he disagreed quite radically with many of Bobby Campbell's ideas.

The two of them fell out, and when Bobby decided to drop Terry from the team after only ten matches it created a terrible split in the dressing-room. Some of the players felt Cooper was out of order to so openly question the manager. Others felt he was right and they wanted his ideas and experience to be made more use of. It all had a devastating effect on the team and the results began to go into a spin.

At the same time there was more friction in the club at boardroom level because the old division between the interests of the stadium company and the football club was breaking open.

Negotiations about a new lease were going painfully slowly. Con Stevens and his son Ian were trying to cement their control of the football club, and Con wanted Ian to become chairman. Ian too wanted the job. But the other directors felt that the Stevens family could end up negotiating with themselves to put far too much money into the Stadium company and their own pockets rather than provide a fair lease. There was also a lot of redevelopment work likely to be needed and again there were arguments over who should pay.

Now if the board were divided over these issues, they also couldn't agree on which side of the fence to put their weight in the arguments between Bobby Campbell and Terry Cooper. But they did know that with Rovers sliding deep into relegation trouble as Christmas approached, something had to change. So Campbell was relieved of his management duties and returned to the role of chief scout. But instead of siding with Cooper they simply went for a good old-fashioned English compromise and put youth coach Harold Jarman in charge for the rest of the season instead.

HAROLD JARMAN

H AROLD JARMAN'S appointment was by no means a unanimous agreement. There was actually only one vote in it on the motion to sack Bobby Campbell. I won't name the director who told me that because I've always tried to keep the secrets I've been told while pouring drinks in the boardroom, but I do know that he regretted it later because he wasn't a fan of Cooper either.

Yet while the decision might have been borne out of compromise, it was actually inspired. If anybody had the ability to heal all the wounds of the rows that had been happening behind the scenes, Harold was the man. He was, and still is, so laid back himself that he found it easy to change the atmosphere and get everybody enjoying their football again.

He was also a man the fans could get behind, because throughout his time as a player he had been a firm favourite. From 1959 until 1973 he had been a stalwart of the side, with his tricky dribbling skills and firm shooting with both feet. He actually got 127 goals from 440 League appearances which is quite a sensational figure for a winger. And he was also a successful cricketer – one of those people from a bygone age who played football and cricket at top level.

Between 1961 and 1971 he starred for Rovers in the winter and then chipped in a few runs for Gloucestershire in the summer. And with the number of Rovers fans who followed the fortunes of the cricket club at the County Ground he became a bit of a cult hero.

He had actually gone away to play for New York Cosmos after leaving Rovers, and always told anybody who would listen that his claim to fame was being replaced by Pele in the team before he came back to England! Bobby Campbell gave him the job as youth coach in 1978, and so he knew well many of the younger players who were now so important to the first team.

Gordon Bennett's work in South Wales had seen him progress to become youth officer, and he'd worked closely with Harold setting up what was called the Bristol Parkway project. Roy Dolling was heavily involved too in what was an imaginative scheme to get round the FA rules. You see professional clubs at that time weren't allowed to be involved with schoolboys, and the only way around it was to start up another club under a different name. So Bristol Parkway became Rovers' nursery club and out at Hambrook on a Sunday morning the youngsters of all ages would play one game after another. It was much like the centres of excellence which are run now, except we could never officially acknowledge that it was anything to do with us!

Now at 40 years old Harold had the club in his heart and was determined to rescue them and at the same time prove his own potential as a manager. Harold's first move was to bring Cooper back from the cold. After all how could a team who were struggling to avoid relegation at the foot of the Second Division possibly not find room for a World Cup legend? Jarman's idea was to play him as a sweeper, with the rest of the team marking man for man, and it worked superbly. Cooper played out of his skin because he was equally determined to show that he should get the manager's job, and slowly the results came together well enough to edge into 19th place at the end of the season and safety.

Harold also spotted the potential of Gary Mabbutt who he had worked with in the youth teams. Of course Harold had played with Gary's father Ray, so he had known Gary well from when he was tiny. He also knew how determined the young Gary was to make it as a professional footballer and prove he was the equal of his elder brother.

That was Kevin Mabbutt, who had been on Bristol City's books and earmarked as a starlet from a very young age. He was a goalscorer with natural flair and with City at that time in the First Division under Alan Dicks, Kevin was enjoying all the attention and adulation you could ask for. Gary, meanwhile, was considered not to have the same natural talent. Yet he did have a talent for hard work, practising for hours on end to develop his skills, and I don't have to tell you which of the two boys ended up having the most distinguished career, do I?

Harold also found another young man by the name of Mickey Barrett, who looked the least like a footballer of anybody you'd see. He was round shouldered and gangling but a superb winger. Well I say Harold found him, because I don't think I ever met any of the senior management at that time who didn't claim to be the person who first spotted Barrett playing for Shirehampton in an amateur tournament to which Rovers had also sent a team. Harold said he found him, so did Terry Cooper, and Bobby Campbell claimed it too. So, for that matter, did Bill Dodgin. Uncle Tom Cobbley would also have got in on the act if he'd been at Eastville at the time!

Harold got the atmosphere at the training ground – and on the bus to away matches – full of smiles again and it was certainly a happy time for me as I settled into my new job. I was beginning to find out what it was like looking after the kit for a club that effectively didn't have a home ground. Even for Eastville matches I had to move all the gear from Hambrook down the M32 to the stadium. It really was an away game every week, and that pattern wasn't going to change for the next 22 years.

Taking the stuff to Eastville wasn't as easy as you might think, either, because of a growing division between the stadium company and the football club.

On Fridays before a home game I had to take all the gear down to lay it out in the dressing-room ready for the next day. I had treated myself to a big Volvo car with part of my redundancy money, and that was perfect because I could load all the big skips and wicker baskets full of shirts, shorts, socks, pads and boots and drive them down the M32 to Eastville Stadium.

Friday was market day at Eastville, so you couldn't go into the His Majesty's entrance and had to make your way through the Muller Road End. Somehow once we'd got there nobody could then ever find the key to the dressing-rooms and I used to have to clamber up the fire escape, jump across to the stand, and then go down and open the dressing-room up from inside. They didn't want us there, and they made their feelings known by being as awkward as they could.

Despite all those problems we collected enough results to stay up, despite the final scare of losing the last two matches and winning only one game in April. Even so Harold had carried out his short term mission to secure Second Division survival, and thought he would then get the job permanently. But his hopes were dashed as the power in the boardroom was shifting again and shortly after the season was over Terry Cooper was installed as manager.

I don't think Harold ever quite got over the disappointment of not being allowed to keep the job he loved. He left that summer to become chief scout at Blackburn, and even when he came back to Rovers a few years later to take over for a second spell as youth coach there was more upset to come. When in 1986 all the costs were being cut to keep the club alive, Harold was among those who were made redundant.

TERRY COOPER

I'LL always believe that Terry Cooper could have been one of Bristol Rovers' better managers. Sadly it seemed every card was stacked against him.

At the time Terry was given the job, the rift between the stadium company and the football club at boardroom level was growing more and more bitter. There were also divisions within the football side of the club where long-serving Rovers men resented the arrival of an ex-Bristol City player in charge. And then to top it all came the South Stand fire. In hindsight poor Terry never really stood a chance.

The boardroom problems had been growing since the 1960s as the stadium owners argued over the level of rent that Rovers should pay – and the contribution the football club should give to ground improvements. In fact you could probably trace their roots to just after the war.

You'll remember that the club had been sold back in 1939 to Con Stevens and his greyhound racing company for just £12,000. Well as Rovers battled to get back on their feet in peacetime, Mr Stevens, together with his company's managing director John Hare, offered to put another £3,000 into the football club by doubling its share capital and loaning a further £1,500. So they duly acquired a controlling interest, and then took the positions of chairman and vice chairman to gain control of both football club and stadium.

That lasted only until 1950, however, because shortly after Bert Tann took over both Stevens and Hare had been relieved of their positions following an FA inquiry into alleged irregular expense payments. They also instructed the greyhound company to dispose of its controlling interest in the football club. They did this by means of Mr Hare selling the 400 shares he held as the greyhound company's nominee to himself as a private individual. So the seeds of mistrust and discontent were sown, even though both Stevens and Hare were more than 100 per cent committed to Rovers.

By the 1970s the problems were growing worse. Douglas Mearns Milne, who had been chairman for many years, was preparing to stand down and as I have said before Con Stevens wanted his son Ian to take over. In the event Graham Holmes, who had come through the ranks of the Presidents Club, was installed as a compromise together with solicitor Alan Seager. But that didn't stop the wrangling going on.

Terry's appointment was certainly not unanimous. If only one vote had removed Bobby Campbell, then the decision not to give the job to Harold Jarman was also probably pretty close. But he did have the support of Holmes and Seager. And he set about the task with enthusiasm and ambition.

For a start Terry persuaded the directors to think big and go into the transfer market. He brought giant centre-forward Bob Lee for £70,000 from Sunderland, paid another £50,000 to Derby for centre-half Aiden McCaffery, and £50,000 more to Bristol City for Scottish defender Donnie Gillies. With his former Leeds team mate Clive Middlemass arriving as his coach, and a fully-qualified physio in Dave Caines appointed to provide a higher standard of treatment for injuries while Wayne Jones was still qualifying and taking exams, Terry was ready to go.

The season opened on 16 August with a 1-1 draw against Orient with David Williams scoring, and the mood was good. A day later it all changed.

I had gone down to Bournemouth for the day, and returned home at tea-time full of the joys of spring having had a wonderful day out. Then somebody asked: "Haven't you heard? Rovers ground has burned down." I dashed down there to find out more, and discovered the old South Stand, home of all our dressing-rooms, kit store and offices, was burned to the ground.

They say to this day it was an electrical fire, which started in the room where all the fuses were housed behind the glass enclosure at the Tote End of the ground. And because it was a Sunday, and the market was going through its usual busy hustle and bustle in the car parks, the fire engines couldn't get access quickly enough to do anything about it. It was also an old wooden Victorian structure, and the moment it caught light it went up in no time. Thinking back to it you think also of the horror that followed a few years later in Bradford, where the ferocious flames spread through a similar wooden structure just as quickly. You think it was at least a small mercy that this blaze didn't happen a day earlier when it could have had just the same tragic consequences.

Bobby Campbell had been at Eastville when the blaze began. After losing his job as manager he had stayed to do scouting and was also working assisting the physios, and he had gone in there to look after some injured players. They had gone home but he was still there tidying up, and together with director Graham Hole they rescued as much of the kit as they could. Gordon Bennett who had just been promoted from youth coach to club secretary was also, typically, in and working on that Sunday morning and he helped too. Together they brought out all the playing gear they could from the burning stand and piled it all on to the pitch (a really big job as you can appreciate).

Now we faced a real crisis, with one half of the ground burned down and closed, and no dressing-rooms or boardroom. And if the boardroom atmosphere had been smouldering with mistrust before that fateful Sunday, it also went up in flames. The stand had in any case been waiting to undergo a safety inspection which would surely have meant money needed to be spent on it. I remember one angry director presenting Ian Stevens with a letter before the next board meeting which effectively accused him of starting the fire deliberately. Ian had been at the ground when it started, but at the crucial time the blaze began had taken his dog for a walk to the far side of the stadium car park so that the first signs of trouble weren't noticed and the blaze had taken hold before the alarm could be raised. Clark Osborn, the stadium manager, also had the finger pointed at him. In both cases, of course, that was malicious and unfair because the fire investigations people clearly pinpointed an electrical fault. But it didn't stop the arguments which raged at the next Rovers board meeting.

Meanwhile the team had to cope with the practical problems. It was probably no wonder that we lost 4-0 at Queen's Park Rangers a couple of days later, but then a 0-0 draw against Bristol City raised our hopes again. The trouble was we didn't have a ground to play on because burned out Eastville wasn't safe. And so an agreement was made to share at Ashton Gate on a temporary basis.

If anybody has ever wondered if it would work for the two Bristol clubs to go to one ground, the answer came in those few weeks. Rovers fans simply wouldn't go to Ashton Gate. It was "enemy" territory to them, and the crowds hit an all-time low, with barely 3,000 watching a goalless draw with Oldham and then just 5,000 – many of them visiting fans – to watch another 0-0 draw with Newcastle.

The club simply had to get back to Eastville. Without the benefit of a genuine home advantage the results were already sliding and a relegation fight was about to begin.

As the relatively new kit man I was beginning to be introduced to the idea that I would never have a home ground, either. Dave Caines was giving me a great insight into all my new duties, but they were already becoming more than the average kit man has to cope with! We moved the entire base of the club out to Hambrook, and suddenly instead of being a football club we were like Billy Smart's Circus – always on the move! In fact it was almost easier when we went away – at least then the team coach would drive into Hambrook so I could load on all the skips and baskets full of boots.

When we were at home my big Volvo had to come to the rescue again, with everything being bundled into the boot and the back seat to drive across to Ashton Gate and then later the shorter trip down the road to Eastville. Little did I know that before long we would be off to Bath with it all instead!

Gordon Bennett's ability to organise and think his way round any problem was vital. How, after all, could you start playing matches at a stadium which had no dressing-room? The answer was simple for Gordon. The teams both changed at Hambrook, then got on to their two coaches and drove down the M32 to the ground. And after they simply got back on to the bus and returned to the Hambrook training ground – then showered in some spare rooms loaned to us by the Crest hotel next door!

Quite what the players of Cambridge and Sheffield Wednesday thought of that I don't know, but at least by the time of our next home League game with West Ham we had installed Portakabin changing rooms beside the Muller Road terrace. There were three of them, with the teams changing either side and using the shower area in the middle. By the time it was dark after the game, however, the cabins became almost transparent and everybody got a perfect view from outside of the likes of Billy Bonds and Trevor Brooking as God made them! Thankfully it wasn't too long before dressing-rooms were installed on the ground floor of the North Stand – and very nice they were too.

You might have hoped that the problems would have upset our opponents and helped Rovers win some home games. The reverse happened because it seemed to make any of our visitors even more determined to take some points home from their grotty day out. And slowly the results began to get worse and worse. It was 4 November before we won a game in the League.

Poor Bob Lee, hailed as the star centre-forward, was having a nightmare. At least in a game at Chelsea he finally got on the scoresheet – trouble was it was in his own net. We had battled through about 80 minutes and McCaffery got up to head away what seemed to be Chelsea's 100th corner! Lee, about five yards outside

Rovers' penalty area, went to clear it further by hooking it over his head – and instead managed to strike it crisply on the volley back past a helpless Martin Thomas from 25 yards!

I don't think Terry was helped by the backbiting that was going on behind the scenes among the Rovers' old guard who were still involved. Bill Dodgin had fallen out with him over their differing views on training methods. Bill also hated the fact that he was an ex Bristol City player. And he hated even more that Terry had been involved in Don Revie's great Leeds team, quite why I will never know.

People like Joe Davis, Mike Lyons and Bobby Jones all drifted away from the scene because they resented being bossed by a Bristol City man. Looking back it was petty because Terry had a wealth of experience and some great ideas, but there's no doubt it happened.

His answer was to work to build a new team spirit among the people who were at the club. He was firm but fair, and a superb coach. And he encouraged the younger players who were emerging through the youth ranks. Welsh youth international Mark Hughes became a regular at centre-half, Geraint Williams was introduced to midfield, and a young midfielder called Ian Holloway also got his debut. Another from the Welsh academy, Neil Slatter, became the youngest player in the club's history when he had his first game at the age of just 16 years and 314 days.

Terry had a talent for encouraging the youngsters – and nobody benefited more than a young man who was to become one of the greats of the game. Gary Mabbutt had emerged under Bobby Campbell as a fine talent, but was now establishing himself as a player of genuine quality. His character was also glowing through.

Poor Gary, the least talented of the Mabbutt brothers, was already in Kevin's shadow. He also had to deal with the break up of the parents he loved. And then he was taken ill and diagnosed as diabetic. His reaction was typical. When his distraught Dad Ray went to see him in hospital, Gary simply told him: "Don't worry Dad, I'll be the first diabetic to play for England." And of course he was right.

Gary was desperate to work and to learn, and in Terry he had the perfect man to learn from. I think even now Gary would name TC as one of the guiding lights to his fabulous career. They spent hours out on the training ground when the others had gone with one-to-one tuition. How to kick with the inside of the foot, the outside of the foot, how to head the ball, how to take a corner accurately. All of Terry's training sessions were first class, and Gary lapped up all the information he could, with his father pushing him all the way to succeed.

Meanwhile Terry's wife Rosemary also got involved in nurturing the family atmosphere, organising a creche for the players' wives and making sure that everybody felt they belonged. The part of the South Stand which hadn't been burned down had now been knocked down for ground safety, but slowly the Coopers built an attitude which made you feel the club was special even if we only had half a ground!

He was also ably assisted by Clive Middlemass who was a superb right hand man. Clive, who is now successful chief scout at Preston, was so dedicated and thorough in everything he did and was also an outstanding coach. It was no surprise to me that the pair of them were later so successful together at Bristol City and then Birmingham.

On Saturday nights after home games I used to go out with Terry, Rosemary and their three young children together with Alan Seager and his family, and Clive and his kids. It was like a party – although I was always late because I had to load all the kit back into my Volvo and take the dirty washing to the house of a lady called Esme Grinham who lived in Southmead. From there all the other playing gear had to be returned to the training ground at Hambrook. It would often take me a couple of hours to sort it all out, but never once did they start the meal until I got there.

It was about this time that Barry Bradshaw, a self made businessman who had built himself a small fortune importing this new fangled gadget called a microwave oven, came on to the board. And he very quickly donated one of his ovens to be installed on the coach for away trips. My job now became not just kit manager but matchday chef, sorting out a proper cooked meal for every player on the way home after games.

Sounds easy when you think about a modern microwave oven, doesn't it? Back in 1980 they weren't quite so reliable and it was very hit and miss. Quite often the power surges the oven needed would overload the coach generator.

John Harding, who then and now works so hard for the Presidents club, would supply me every week free of charge with 30 pieces of braising steak ready for the journey. I would then go to buy all the vegetables, take the lot home and spend Friday night cooking. The steak could be braised on Friday, and then I'd get up at the crack of dawn or a long way before to get the vegetables sorted. Then they had to be served on paper and plastic plates and packed into sealed boxes, along with apple tart and custard plus cheese and biscuits, put again into my Volvo, and driven off to Hambrook ready to load on to the coach.

After the game the players would board the coach and all have a starter of either soup or prawn cocktail – and then take turns four at a time at the table to eat the meals as each one was cooked. Well the oven drained loads of power from the coach and sometimes didn't work and left it cold, and at other times overcooked it. In any case it was a new gadget so we were all learning about how best to make it work. To make matters more difficult you could only cook one meal at a time and there always seemed to be a squabble among the players on who would eat first.

When we were playing at York with a four-hour journey it wasn't too big a problem to cook the meals one after the other for a squad of 14 or 15 players plus the directors and staff. If we were nearer home in Birmingham there were still one or two hungry by the time we got back to Bristol!

The other problem for me was one of simply balancing to stand still at the back of a coach that was travelling down a bumpy road at 80 miles an hour, to make sure I could dish up the dinners without spilling the gravy. My knees were still bobbing up and down like a skier when I got off the coach back at home! But at least I think everybody enjoyed my menu – and Dave Caines and Roy Dolling used to serve at the tables with equal care!

As the year turned and the results still failed to arrive, the supporters club raised the money to bring Paul Randall back from Stoke for £50,000. He had scored enough goals to get Stoke promotion, but then hadn't enjoyed much success at the Victoria Ground in a higher division, and seemed to be the answer to everybody's prayers as he came back to get two goals in a 2-1 win over Bolton on his home debut. Sadly that was a false dawn, and Rovers finished up the season in bottom place with only five League wins to their credit all season. All the work that Don Megson put in to gain Second Division status a few years before had almost literally all gone up in flames.

The summer saw the next stage of the boardroom revolution, as the Stevens family lost their grip on the club. Barry Bradshaw, together with Graham Hole and Martin Flook, successfully staged the same sort of remarkable share coup that had handed the Stevens family their controlling interest all those years earlier.

They engineered an extraordinary meeting one night at the Crest Hotel to agree an extra £75,000 of share capital in a rights issue. They knew the Stevens family couldn't afford to take up their rights. Martin Flook, a businessman from Portishead who had made his money selling air-conditioning systems to the Arabs, was waiting to buy control. But to push the plan through they first had to be able to outvote Con and Ian Stevens in a poll vote. So they almost literally dug up every shareholder they could find to join the campaign, tracking down people who had owned one or two shares and finding their relatives who in many cases didn't even know they had inherited them. Their campaign was a success, and that summer Flook proudly took the helm as the club's new chairman.

His money, together with Barry Bradshaw, had helped finance the signing of Randall and the two men were clearly the new power at the club. Before long they would be the only joint chairmen in the League.

The new season started with another folk hero pulled out of nowhere – a painter and decorator called Archie Stephens who was playing in the Western League for Melksham. Archie, a lovely lad from Liverpool, burst on to the scene with two goals in both his first two full games and with his powerful style and strength in the air Rovers had a hit. He had a broad scouse accent, and could he rabbit on. He had an answer for everything, although it always began with him stuttering: "But, but, but" before putting his point of view. But his character made him hugely popular with the rest of the lads. He came from a big family, and when we played at Tranmere they all came to watch him. When the coach turned the corner of the road into Prenton Park we could see I think four Archie Stephens lookalikes stood on the corner – and the mood of the team was that we should sign them all up!

Terry's other two signings that summer were top quality. He brought Brian Williams, a tenacious little left-back who was built like a lightweight boxer and had a fiery streak to his character, from Swindon in a swop deal for midfield man Gary Emmanuel. And at centre-half came Tim Parkin.

Tim was signed after Terry followed up an enquiry about an English centre-half who had been playing for Malmö in Sweden. Just a year earlier that club had been playing against Forest in the European Cup final, and after checking his pedigree Terry gambled on the bargain £15,000 fee.

He asked me to drive him up to Heathrow to meet Timmy, and we successfully made it to Terminal One where the flight from Sweden was due to arrive. As the first people landed, however, our manager decided he had to go and answer a call of nature and left me to meet this new player.

"How will I recognise him?" I asked.

"No problem," Terry reassured me. "He's 6ft 2ins tall, blond, and built like a man mountain. You can't miss him."

So that was good. Except that the flight was from Sweden and as nearly 200 people came through the arrivals door they were all 6ft 2ins tall, blond, and built like a man mountain!

Thankfully it was Tim who shortly afterwards recognised Terry, and we brought our man back to Bristol where he went on to play for the next five seasons.

The season started well – with another new kid Phil Kite in goal saving a penalty in a 3-1 win at Exeter that took us briefly to the top of the table. And there were still no real signs of problems despite a one- goal defeat at Southend in early October. Then came the weekend when Terry's blunt Yorkshire honesty let him talk himself out of a job.

We played Swindon at home, and suffered one of those nightmare days when everybody played badly at the same time, and Swindon got everything right. In front of a crowd of nearly 9,000 we lost 4-1.

Terry, full of disappointment, came up into the boardroom area a good hour and a half after the final whistle and sat down between Martin Flook and Barry Bradshaw. Martin turned to him and asked: "What happened today, then?"

Terry just smiled and said: "What a silly question. It's obvious what happened. We were rubbish. We couldn't put two passes together and we didn't deserve to win. In fact we were f*****g hopeless."

That was about the end of the conversation, and I thought little more of it. It was the sort of assessment you'd hear many managers make at different times. But Martin clearly took exception to the verdict and by next morning had organised a meeting of all the directors out at Hambrook which voted for Terry to get the sack. I'm convinced to this day that if Terry had just given some sort of made-up technical explanation for the defeat and created a story about Swindon's clever tactics he'd have kept his job.

Instead through being honest we were back to square one with no manager again. And to make it, in my view, an even sadder day for the club Clive Middlemass went as well. The directors were in a position where they had to act fast – and that's exactly what they did.

BOBBY GOULD

BOBBY Gould had two spells as manager at Bristol Rovers. What most people don't know is that the first of them very nearly lasted less than a day.

After making his sudden decision to axe Terry Cooper, Martin Flook moved quickly to sort out a successor. We played at Oxford a couple of days later, and while the team were enjoying their pre-match meal at a hotel on the edge of town, Flook and Barry Bradshaw together with Graham Holmes and Alan Seager left them for a secret rendezvous with the man they had identified as their next boss.

Since his departure from Eastville just three years earlier, Bobby had done the rounds learning his management trade. In a whirlwind move up the career ladder, he had been to Hereford as player-coach, then on to Wimbledon and then Chelsea as player-coach, and was now player-coach again at Aldershot. Significantly he had also kept his home and settled with wife Marjorie and his two boys Jonathan and Richard in Portishead throughout that time, just a few miles from Flook's own house.

Coming back to Bristol to take his first management post was a dream move for him, and the talks were simple and straightforward. The following day his appointment was announced.

Within hours of taking over, however, he resigned. He'd accepted a sensible salary to grab his first chance of being a boss, and was then furious to find out that most of the senior players were earning more than him! He asked for a rise, was turned down, and so simply walked out. The directors were in a corner and backed down, quickly changing the situation to give him what he wanted. Where Bert Tann once kept the job for 17 years, Bobby wouldn't have managed 17 hours! But it was an important point of principle for him, and it set the tone for how he wanted things done his way. Bobby was a great showman who wanted to project himself and the club. He felt that if Rovers got publicity it would help attract the crowds and he worked hard to make sure the local papers had plenty to write about.

He wanted high standards of presentation, and he certainly set them for himself. Very often he'd wear three different tracksuits in one morning's training. I remember he had dug around the rooms at Eastville where Bobby Campbell would store kit. Now Bobby was a bit of a hoarder, and was always putting some extra gear aside in case it was needed later. It wasn't a bad principle as I learned myself in the years that followed to make sure there was always some spare shirts, shorts and training wear if you suddenly had a couple of new signings half way through the season.

Bobby Campbell, however, took this to extremes – and Gouldy found about 16 complete sets of playing kit stretching back over the best part of a decade! He got it all out for use in training, and I think at times we had better gear to train in than to play.

Bob's old West Ham team mate John McDowell came from Norwich as player-coach. Now John had played 240 games for the Hammers and another season at Carrow Road, and was just the sort of experienced defender that would have been an asset in Division Three. It quickly became clear, however, as he limped through the cross country training runs that he was never going to be fit enough to carry out the player part of his duties. His right leg limped terribly, and John concentrated instead on guiding the crop of promising youngsters at the club. His reserve sides always played wonderful simple attacking football that could be a joy to watch.

Poor Bob was quickly to learn that appointing staff was one of the more difficult aspects of management. His next player-coach half way through the season was Garry Pendrey, a likeable defender from Birmingham who is still in the game now as Gordon Strachan's number two at Coventry. Garry played just one game for Rovers, though, with more injury problems keeping him sidelined before he gave up driving down the M5 and took a job at Walsall instead.

Bobby had a totally different style to Terry Cooper, and it caused some friction among the players. Where Terry had been laid back and relaxed as a character, Bob would grow more and more intense as the week went on and then by Saturday was worked up into a lather.

He cared passionately about the job he was doing, and he expected the players to have the same sort of focus and couldn't understand that it didn't always happen. I think it's a fact of football life that players, simply because they are younger, tend to drift along taking much of what happens to them for granted and it is only a rare few that have the same sort of drive and ambition as their boss.

Bobby tried to stamp his authority, banning the playing of cards on the coach after we'd reached the pre-match hotel. He told them they should concentrate their minds totally on the game in front of them. For the most part, however, the little card school at the back of the coach concentrated instead on how to hide the pack of cards and the hands that were still being dealt out underneath the table!

There was one away trip to Swindon at the beginning of March when we headed down the M4 through pouring rain, and in front of us emerged the most amazing spectacle. Three high-powered police motorway patrol cars were chasing a Reliant Robin. It was before *Only Fools and Horses* had begun to be a hit show, but really Del Boy himself couldn't have driven this little three-wheeler with more daring. Every time one of the police cars moved alongside it, the Robin swerved and refused to be stopped. The chase lasted for 10 or 15 minutes with all the players crowding to the front of the coach watching the action as we followed 100 yards behind. Eventually the man in the Reliant Robin tried one manoeuvre too many and crashed spectacularly into the central barrier with lumps of fibreglass flying everywhere. We drove on past with Bobby shouting desperately at the players: "Sit down, don't look, concentrate on the game, forget this." We ended up losing 5-2!!

On another occasion we were thrashed 4-0 at Burnley, and Bobby changed his mind about giving permission for Brian Williams to stay in Lancashire for the weekend with his parents. There was a furious row and Brian refused to travel back home – but I think it cost him a heavy fine when he got in on Monday!

Another heavy away defeat that year was at Plymouth, where again we lost 4-0. Bobby bundled everybody on to the coach 20 minutes after the final whistle, and refused to let anybody have any food. I was forbidden from serving the normal microwave meals, and the orders were that everybody had to starve and think about how badly they had played. Well that was all very well except that poor Gary Mabbutt, because of his diabetes, was under doctors orders that he must eat as soon as possible after matches and we ended up smuggling biscuits back to him at the back of the bus!

I hope none of those stories give the wrong impression of Bobby, because the truth was that his passion and enthusiasm were vital qualities that made a big difference at the club. He believed in everything being done along totally professional lines, and had a very methodical way of working things out. If he had a problem to think through he would deal with that and that alone until he felt he'd solved it, and then go on to the next one.

He felt strongly that the club was in danger of losing its roots as more and more of the office administration got done from the Portakabin at the Hambrook training ground, and he insisted that space was found in the North Stand at Eastville to create new offices for us. Marjorie Hall brought her feminine touch to getting those fitted out, with giant mirrors everywhere in the tiny, dark rooms and corridors to create an illusion of space. It looked good, but it did encourage physio Wayne Jones to perform a very good Harry Worth impression every time he was there.

Marjorie swiftly fell out of favour, however, when she failed to meet Bob's high standards of professionalism.

We had brought through the ranks a young midfielder from Knowle called Steve Bailey, who was still only 17 when he made his debut and bristled with promise. On his 18th birthday he duly signed professional forms – but Marjorie, who was under immense pressure with so much work to do, failed to register the new contract with the Football League. By the time anybody realised, Steve had played another game and Rovers had technically breached the rules. The club was docked two points for fielding an ineligible player, and Bobby was rightly furious. Douglas Mearns Milne and Bert Brown saved her job even though she did the decent thing and offered to resign. But the relationship between manager and assistant secretary became so frosty that Marjorie didn't stay much longer.

Bobby finished his first season under pressure, really. Terry had been sacked because Rovers drifted out of the top two or three promotion places, and we ended up only finishing as high as 15th because we won the last two games. But it had been a good learning curve for him, and he soon showed he would benefit.

In the summer he sold Mabbutt to Tottenham for £100,000, which was a good piece of business then. And it seemed his next signings – two lads from non-League football called Nicky Platnauer and Graham Withey – didn't signal too much ambition. But as the season got under way Bob found a flair for bringing in huge star players which lifted Rovers' profile and got people flocking to see the club again.

The first to come was Mike Channon, 34 years old and drifting towards the end of his fantastic 46-cap career. After leaving South-ampton and going to Hong Kong, he had then joined Newcastle but found the First Division a bit too tough and was released on a free transfer. Bobby, who had played with Channon at The Dell, rang and asked if he fancied keeping himself fit by signing for Rovers. It was a great coup, and a team who started the season getting barely 3,000 for a home crowd suddenly brought in double that.

Typical of Bobby he then left Channon on the subs bench for a couple of games because his team had put together two four-goal victories and he wasn't going to change a winning side!

Mickey was a lovely lad who mixed into the dressing-room with no airs and graces, chatting with that unmistakable Hampshire accent. He'd arrive on match days and go straight to the North Stand to watch the racing on TV, and give me a bundle of money every day to look after while he was training. He gave me a few good horse racing tips as well, and several of the lads had some good investments backing horses with the win bonuses they were earning at the time.

Bobby had all sorts of strict rules and regulations, one of which was that players were not allowed to cut their toenails on a matchday. John Higgins, who worked for a while as physio, was very keen on all those different codes and was furious one day when he walked in about an hour before kick-off and found Mickey clipping his nails. John started to lay down the law to Channon, who simply looked at him and said: "When you've played as many games as I have you can tell me what to do".

Mickey didn't stay more than six weeks – but before long we had another new arrival with even more England caps. Alan Ball, who had just lost his job as manager at Blackpool and again was looking for a place to play and get fit while he picked his career up again.

Ironically while the public loved Gould's ability to deliver big names, within the dressing-room it wasn't so popular. The younger players felt they were being kept out of the side unfairly, and that their progress was being held back by these ageing superstars. I remember Ian Holloway in particular being furious at Ball's arrival because it cost him his place in the team. Years later he was to admit how wrong he was – and how much he'd learned from being in the same club as an England World Cup winner.

The biggest problem we had with Alan was that he normally took his own car to away matches to meet us. I normally had to take it and park it once he'd met the coach at the pre-match hotel, and everybody seemed both to recognise his red mercedes and to want to pinch the badge off the bonnet!

Once we played at Exeter and I had to park it in the streets – and I didn't spot the sign that said "Permit Holders Only". When he came out after the game there was a ticket with a £25 fine slapped on the windscreen. Gouldy sorted it out and paid it from his own pocket within five minutes because he knew it was my mistake and he wouldn't let his player suffer for it. And really that was typical of Bob, because while he expected players to give their all he made sure he gave everything back. He would know the birthdays of their wives and send flowers, and he fussed over their families.

He was also a sly old fox. For a while he moved training to Eastville Park on a couple of days a week, and would get the players to jog down there while John McDowell started the training sessions off. Bobby would follow in his car – and then hide and watch from a distance to see who worked properly when they didn't think the boss was watching and who tried to slack off.

Slowly the atmosphere around the club had been rebuilt. The old players like Mike Lyons and Joe Davis were coming back to help with the Parkway teams. And the youngsters coming through were thriving as they learned the ropes from great England stars. The results weren't quite good enough so that any chance of promotion was slipping away, but the away support was brilliant and the club vibrant.

So Gordon Bennett came up with a wonderful idea to reward the fans who were getting behind the team so well. In mid-April we were due to play Walsall, a short trip up the M5, and he put together an offer of free coach travel for any fans who went to cheer on the team in their last efforts to get back in the promotion places.

It was a clever scheme. In those days the visiting club got half the gate money, so while it cost around £3 a head to lay on the free coach we got £3.50 back from Walsall. The club would make money while appearing to give the fans something for nothing. It was the sort of scheme that Gordon was so clever at producing.

He couldn't have imagined, though, quite how successful it would be. Every coach from all over the West Country ended up being commandeered for the great expedition with nearly 2,000 fans making the trip.

Well we set off earlier than the fans, and went to the hotel before going on to Fellows Park at about 1.30. Bobby, Roy Dolling and myself went to set out the kit – and Bob took one look at the dressing-room and walked back out in disgust. It was so dirty he wouldn't let the players go in, and so they had to stay on the bus with John McDowell talking to them while we tried to sort things out. Roy and I got on our hands and knees and mopped the room out ourselves, while Bobby went off to have a ruck with Walsall's manager about the state of it all. In fairness to them I think it was a genuine mistake – there had been a reserve game earlier in the day and somebody had forgotten to get the cleaning duties done. But that didn't stop Bob having a slanging match, before rolling his sleeves up to help clean out the large plunge bath before the boys arrived.

They say in football you get out what you put in – and Walsall were so wound up by it all that they came out in a fury. We lost 5-0. There was another ruck after the game as Gouldy walked into the dressing-room, ordered everybody on the bus in 20 minutes, and warned there would be a fine of a week's wages for those that missed it!

What Bobby wanted – and got – was for our coach to get caught up in the jam of all the other busses going back so the angry supporters could make the players well aware of their fury at such a bad performance. And they did too. The coaches we passed were full of angry fans shaking their fist when they recognised the team bus. We had taken a huge crowd and let them down. Just as happened after that Plymouth game I was told to serve no food, although within a mile of leaving the ground Bob ordered the bus to stop at a McDonalds where he ordered milk shakes for himself, me and Roy Dolling but still made sure nobody else could have a thing. It was fine for us but it didn't make the players too happy! Then when we got back to the hotel at Hambrook nobody was allowed to leave the bus. Bobby began a team meeting there and then which raged on until nearly nine o'clock. Then they were all in for training next day and the inquest went on again.

Bob was so intense on matchdays it hurt. We played at Bradford in the snow and he got in a furious row with their manager Trevor Cherry and the referee beforehand about whether we should use an orange or a white ball. We wanted an orange one which was normal practice on snow, Cherry insisted it should be white. And he also objected to us wearing our all white change colours, so Bob then complained about their gold shirts.

The referee sorted it out. We wore white, they wore gold, and the ball was orange. But with ten minutes to go it was 0-0 when Bradford won a corner, and suddenly the orange ball we were playing with was replaced by a white one which was soft. Within two minutes Bradford scored two goals and Bob was so angry he jumped up and knocked himself out on the roof of the low dug-out. He was furious with Cherry and Terry Yorath afterwards, accusing them of an old Don Revie trick. We had played 85 minutes with orange balls and then lost 2-0 in a couple of minutes with a different coloured one which was also virtually flat.

As the season neared its end and the results slipped away, rumours began to circulate that Coventry had identified Bobby as the man to be their next manager. The chance to go and boss his home town club in the First Division was not one he would turn down. The day before the last game of the season Martin Flook confronted Bobby with the accusation that he was already preparing to go – and sacked him before he had the chance to resign. Bobby, who couldn't be blamed for being ambitious, left Hambrook in tears that his reign as manager should end in such bitterness. And everybody expected Alan Ball to get the job.

Instead it was Ron Gingell, long time manager of Minehead and friend of Flook's from Portishead, who became Bristol Rovers' most unlikely boss ever for a day for the last match of the season against Cardiff.

And after that finished in a 1-1 draw, and I was clearing up the rubbish from the floor once all the players had gone, Martin Flook came into the dressing-room and sat down in between me and Roy Dolling to talk to us.

"Right," he said. "We're going to go out and get a new manager. We'll bring in a new broom to sweep clean. But whatever we do I can assure you we won't have this club managed by a f*****g Welshman!"

So imagine my surprise when within two weeks David Williams was appointed manager with Wayne Jones as his number two!

DAVID WILLIAMS

I F I was surprised at the appointment of David Williams, I should think I was not alone. After all it was fairly common knowledge that Alan Ball applied for the job, and that Larry Lloyd, who by now had achieved great things with Liverpool and Nottingham Forest, was also a serious candidate.

There were many who rubbished the move as a money saving appointment – the outsider in a field of three coming through because he was already there. But in fact it was probably more a case that Martin Flook and Barry Bradshaw were brave enough to back their judgement on the man they rated most highly.

From the moment David first came to the club he had established himself as being a little different to the average player. He was actually still an amateur when he made his debut in 1975, choosing to stay at teacher training college in Cardiff and working in Cardiff's Mostyn High School before he decided to play full time. And he had established his reputation by becoming the youngest ever to qualify as a full badge FA coach. He'd been a regular fixture in the side for eight years, and was as creative and imaginative on the field as he was intelligent and articulate off it. He was also a big friend of Gordon

Bennett because of their links going back to the early days of the Welsh nursery, and when he was interviewed by the directors put his thoughts over with sense and feeling.

At the age of 28 he became not only the youngest manager the club ever had, but the youngest in the entire Football League. But he had a very old head on his shoulders. And with Wayne Jones as his number two he picked a close friend and ally to help him.

David probably kept the most settled side of any Rovers manager since Bert Tann's early days. He used only 17 players in the whole of his first season despite playing 58 games because the club enjoyed a run to the semi-finals of the newly-created Associate Members Cup. And most of the changes he did make were either due to injuries – or in the case of goalkeeper Phil Kite because he was sold to Southampton for a £50,000 fee. David actually sold two goalkeepers for big money, because he also moved Martin Thomas to Newcastle for £50,000. His only signing in his first summer in charge was to bring Steve White back from Luton for £35,000 – a fraction of the £195,000 record fee that the Hatters had paid in 1979.

Yet David's loyalty to the people he had played alongside before finding himself put in charge of them gained results. In both his seasons as manager Rovers only just missed out on promotion finishing fifth then sixth. In the modern days of the play-offs that might have been good enough. And his quiet, sensible style of management was ideal to help smooth the club through two very sad personal tragedies that touched all our lives.

The first of them befell Timmy Parkin, whose little son John fought a brave three-year battle against leukemia. He and his wife Jane were so proud of their little lad who had been growing up like any other healthy boy until he began to feel ill. A series of tests confirmed their worst fears, and John began to need regular stays at the children's hospital at Frenchay for treatments. It was a long and painful battle, as anybody who has ever been in that sad situation could tell you. Several times the doctors thought the poor little soul might be better – and always the dreadful disease returned.

Yet through it all Timmy continued to turn in superb

performances week in and week out, perhaps because the football field was the one place he could escape his worries for an hour and a half. But when we got back from long away trips he would rush off to join Jane and sit at their little lad's bedside at Bristol Children's Hospital.

After dumping all the gear I used invariably to go with him, and take Jane for long walks to give her a break from the tough vigil she kept while Timmy took his turn to sit beside their son. I remember one night we got back from York, and it was two o'clock in the morning as Jane took me on a tour of the ward. She guided me round, whispering the awful stories: "this little girl has two weeks to live, this boy has a brain tumour, this one may lose a leg." I used to get home and dream about those poor children, and my only comfort was to think that I was helping in some small way.

Sadly John eventually lost his fight too, and I went with David Williams, Wayne Jones and Gordon Bennett up to Appleby in Cumbria which was Tim's home town to attend the funeral, and watch other little boys carrying his coffin.

It was a traumatic affair which put the worries of winning and losing football matches into some context. And then, horribly, came another reminder for us all of the true values of life.

Mickey Barrett had by this time blossomed into a winger of magnificent quality. He had been signed, you'll remember, from non-League football. It had been a bit of a steal on Rovers' part because he'd been offered a trial by Manchester United and had packed up work to get himself fit. Rovers found him in the meantime and offered him a contract that spared him ever going near Old Trafford.

Mike was probably good enough that United would have made use of him. He wasn't quick, or strong, or good in the air. But he just had that old fashioned winger's quality of being able to take the ball up to a defender and then shimmy his body to dump the full-back on his backside before moving away. He crossed the ball superbly with left or right foot, and took one of the most wonderful, inswinging corners you would ever see.

He was a quiet lad, who looked ungainly with slouched shoulders, but he had learned the ways of the full-time game under the guidance of first Terry Cooper and then Bobby Gould, and when David Williams took charge he probably reached his peak. He got 12 goals from the wing in the season, and the longer serving supporters talked of how he was the best winger they had seen since Harold Jarman's great days a couple of decades before.

The rumours were already beginning of which big club might offer a transfer fee that was too good to turn down as we headed for Scotland in the summer of 1984 for a pre-season tour. We stayed at Stirling University in the magnificent campus buildings with wonderful playing fields to train on, and games every other day against Scottish clubs.

But Mickey was struggling to keep up on the pre-season runs, and it was decided to send him back to Bristol to find out why he was ill. They got him back to the Bristol Royal Infirmary where he was diagnosed with cancer. It was already all over his body, and incredibly within two weeks he had died.

It was a massive shock for his wife Louise, who was due to give birth to their son Liam just six weeks later. And it was equally a hammer blow for the whole of the team who couldn't take in the shock. Mike may have been a quiet lad but he was very popular. To this day whenever Brian Williams is in Bristol he makes a point of going to visit Mike's grave at Arnos Vale cemetery. He's just through the gates on the left. Brian at left-back used to love the fact he could just give Mickey the ball and let him get on with beating a defender and putting a cross in, and they were very close.

Perhaps it was because of the feeling of closeness the two tragedies brought to the team, I don't know, but for whatever reason we went off brilliantly with six wins in the first seven games to go top of the League.

A lad called Mark O'Connor had the awesome job of taking over Barrett's left wing role. He was short and nippy and very different in style so the crowd took time to accept him – but by the time he scored the first goal in a 3-1 FA Cup win at Bristol City in December he had certainly won them over.

In the Football League Cup we went to Arsenal, and though we lost 4-0 it was a fascinating look at how the other half lived. The massive dressing-rooms with heated floors had marble everywhere, and in between the home and away room was their medical room which was an absolute showcase. Every modern gadget for the health of a player was in there, and I remember standing there just gobsmacked at the difference to our poor Portakabins back at Hambrook.

Meanwhile our own finances were beginning to bite again, even though David pulled off another good sale by letting Geraint Williams go to Derby for £40,000. Our training base at Hambrook was disrupted because it was let out to the TSB who were sponsoring Bobby Charlton's newly-created soccer schools for ten days. It was a wonderful new idea, and there were hordes of kids running around the place – which gave us another chance to make money for the club by selling them chips, beans and sausages at lunch time. Together with Vi Harris who helped with the washing we did all the cooking for them, and then provided tea and fruitcake in the afternoon. Bobby, incidentally, was magnificent and justified his standing as one of football's legends. He had ten coaches working for him taking a group of children each, and during the day he worked his way around every single one with his great individual help.

While the kids were there it meant our pros had to train somewhere else, and David organised to use the BAWA club in Southmead Road. Before long we began to use it as a regular base while Hambrook got rented out for other people, and the kit man had his workload increased again to take all the training gear to this new venue!

On a Friday especially I had to go to Hambrook early in the day to collect all the training kit to take to the BAWA. At least I had a van to use by this time, but you can imagine the volume of gear to move with 26 sets of track suits and wet weather gear for the players, plus another four or five for the staff. Then there are all the boots, bibs, balls, cones and other bits and pieces. Not just a five-minute job, I can tell you.

Security was a nightmare, so the lads would give me all their valuables which I kept in a bag – and then took away with me while I went back to Hambrook to collect the playing kit which had to be taken to Eastville to be set out ready for the next day. Friday was always a light training morning, so I then had to rush to be back at the BAWA in time to give the lads back all their money, car keys, watches and wallets before they went home. Talk about a rush.

At least the boardroom was lean and efficient after yet another series of coups had left just THREE directors. Martin Flook and Barry Bradshaw were joint chairmen, while Gordon Bennett had been promoted to the title of Managing Director. He was also the Company Secretary. Gordon worked all the hours God gave to organise everything – including for a while the away travel.

Without intending to he fixed up the most chaotic trip ever when we went to Hull in early March. Gordon, whose geography was normally reasonably respectable, slipped up on this occasion because he booked the pre-match meal at the Swallow hotel at South Normanton, some 80 miles or so away from our eventual destination at Boothferry Park.

We got to the hotel successfully, and trooped into the dining room for our rounds of toast, to find that Liverpool were also booked in. They were due to play at Nottingham Forest and having stayed overnight were now tucking into steaks or fish for their sumptuous pre-match meal. All the great players of that era when Liverpool won a succession of European Cups were there – the likes of Ian Rush, Kenny Dalglish, Mark Lawrenson and Bruce Grobbelaar.

Well we politely asked for an autograph or two and then came out to board the bus – only for it not to start. The battery was as flat as a pancake. Our driver asked the Liverpool bus driver to use some heavy duty leads for a jump start. Still there was not a hint of life from the engine. By this time the Liverpool players were coming out to board their bus too, and they joined in as our lads tried to give the coach a push start – still to no avail.

With the clock ticking towards three, and 80 miles still to travel, there was nothing for it but to organise a fleet of taxis. Director

Graham Hole got on the phone and six of them arrived, and I got all the kit out and gave it to each of the players then so they could change on their way. But just to make matters worse there was a new motorway opened to reach Hull, surfaced with loose chippings – and two of the cabs suffered blow-outs on the way.

The four taxis which did make it arrived with a total of nine players – meaning we should be obliged to start the game. So as the referee came to knock on the dressing-room door David thought quickly and ordered three of them to hide in the toilets. As the ref looked round they crouched on top of the pan with the door shut while their manager assured the official that we only had six available players and the rest were on their way! Needless to say we lost the game 2-0. The club received a hefty fine for the late kick-off. And from then on it became my job instead of Gordon Bennett's to fix up the away travel arrangements!

There was another embarrassing trip when we went to Wigan, travelling in a new, luxury bus which had a TV installed. It was a giant screen in a big circular area at the front of the coach which required an equally giant aerial on the front roof of the coach to make it work. We went under the low bridge just outside Wigan's old ground – and got stuck underneath it with the aerial jammed against the bottom of the bridge. That very nearly made us late for kick-off too.

We had our adventures and our fun among the team, but for the directors life was becoming ever more tough. Messrs Flook and Bradshaw tried to buy Eastville Stadium, only to find that Tesco's had got there first and paid a huge chunk of money to build a store at one end. So they tried instead to gain permission for a new ground as part of development at Stoke Gifford, and then tried again on a site near Filton Station.

David, being as shrewd as he was, began to realise that managing the team would only become tougher and his growing reputation as a bright young coach would be damaged if two promotion campaigns suddenly dissolved into a relegation fight. And as the season neared its end he became probably the only player ever to sell himself – agreeing a £40,000 fee to transfer his own registration to Norwich before handing in his resignation as manager.

It was a clever move. He was still only 30, and then enjoyed the best years of his playing career in the First Division before going on to coach again at Carrow Road, then Bournemouth. He's since built a huge reputation as a youth coach, first developing the core of the current Leeds team and then working for Alex Ferguson as the Academy Director at the biggest club in the country.

BOBBY'S BACK!

LARRY Lloyd was again front-runner to become new manager as Rovers' joint chairmen faced up to the most important decision any board can take. He'd just been pipped by David Williams two years earlier, and was still looking for his chance in management.

But the bookies who installed Lloyd as favourite reckoned without the enthusiasm and nerve of Bobby Gould. Two years after walking away in tears with his pride hurt, he came back full of bubbling desire to lead Rovers again in the way that only Bobby could.

In the meantime his dream move to his home town club at Coventry had turned sour. He'd started off by signing a collection of players from the lower divisions – including Nicky Platnauer and Graham Withey from Rovers – and taking the First Division by storm. After a spectacular win over Liverpool he even boasted that he could go into the lower leagues and sign enough players for another five teams just as good.

Sadly his side failed to go on reaching those high standards, and Bobby's matchday passion slowly got the better of him. He was sacked just before Christmas in his second season after storming on to the pitch to confront a referee as a 5-1 defeat at Leicester dumped the Sky Blues right into the relegation mire.

As only Bobby could, he tried a multitude of jobs including cleaning windows while he waited to get back into football – and the Rovers vacancy was just the job for him. He even ate humble pie for the sake of the supporters, admitting he'd been too hasty in leaving Eastville the last time to chase his dreams in the top division before he had been ready.

His early signings didn't bode well for a successful return. He took a boy called Steve Badock from non-League football – and gave him a part-time contract. Badock went on working in Swindon as a British Rail clerk after training had finished. He did score after only two minutes of his debut at Darlington on the first day of the season, and then got two more at Wolves in September. But that was it before he booked himself a one-way ticket back to the part-time game with Gloucester City!

At least Andy Spring, who Bob had known as an apprentice at Coventry, brought some talent. A stocky lad with a shock of blond hair, he was a great entertainer on overnight trips if there was a piano in the hotel. He could play any tune you asked for – and without reading music – and reminded me of the days in Bert Tann's time when Josser Watling used to do the entertaining when the team travelled. He was a brilliant pianist – but unfortunately a hopeless full-back! Fat and overweight, Bob lost patience with him after only half a dozen games by which time we were bottom of the League!

Bob at least hadn't lost his flair for introducing big names to Rovers, enticing former England captain Gerry Francis to become his player-coach. Gerry's arrival was vital for such a young and inexperienced team, and gave them some leadership out on the park.

One week when we suffered a goalkeeping crisis Bob decided to solve it with another big name arrival – asking his close friend Bob Wilson to come out of retirement. Wilson, once an Arsenal legend in their double-winning side, was already beginning to forge his media career by this time. But he was keeping fit by coaching goalkeepers at Highbury, and answered the call to help out his old friend Gould.

His arrival attracted all the media to Hambrook, and the TV cameras were particularly keen to film him in training. In those days as you came out of the Portakabin changing rooms to go on to the pitches there was a white picket fence, with a gate in the middle of it – a bit like the sort of thing you see around an old fashioned cricket pavilion.

The press and TV cameras all wanted the picture of him coming out and opening the gate, but Wilson managed to walk forward and try to push the gate away from him to open it instead of pulling it. To much laughter he went back and tried to take the scene again – only to make the same mistake! I think Bob must have tried the bit of film a dozen times and still got it wrong in each go – before he ended up jumping over it! I'm glad he gets his lines right on TV more easily now! The biggest irony, incidentally, was that Wilson never actually got to play for us – by the end of the week Ron Green was fit and took his usual place between the sticks.

I was glad there wasn't publicity around for another escapade at that time. Hambrook was a quiet place, and late at night the professional girls who worked in the Old Bristol Road used to take their clients up there to conduct their business.

One night I'd come back from Eastville after a night match to store the kit, and when I saw a car parked outside which was rocking slightly I took no notice. I just got the door to my store-room open and carried on with my work. I even paid no attention when I heard the car wheels screech as it drove off at top speed.

But as I carried on offloading the van I heard a faint voice calling: "Please help me". I thought I was dreaming, but heard it again and said: "Come out wherever you are". A young lady of about 18 years old with a red mini skirt that was more like a belt emerged from the night and asked if I could help. She'd had a problem with a client and had been beaten up. I told her I would call the police, but she begged me not to and gave me another number to call instead. It was obviously her pimp. I got given instructions to drop her at Frenchay hospital where somebody would pick her up, and because it was so late I agreed to do as I was asked.

When I told the story next day the lads pulled my leg over and over again. But it turned out to have a serious side because at about that time the police were hunting for the person who had murdered a prostitute in the Old Bristol Road. And one day they suddenly turned up at the training ground and insisted I went with them to be interviewed. For two hours I was interrogated as if I was a suspect in the murder inquiry, and it wasn't a pleasant experience I can tell you.

Mind you, Hambrook was also used by courting couples who were making love for its own sake rather than for money. And several times when the coach drew up late at night after an away trip the lads would quietly creep up on a discreetly parked car and then start rocking it before going away in fits of laughter.

Gouldy might have been working on the club's public image, but behind the scenes the financial crisis was getting deeper and deeper. The obvious signs had been there before the season even began when Martin Flook and Barry Bradshaw quit as joint chairmen. I thought they both deserved some credit. Flook had promised when he first took over that if he couldn't move Rovers into a new home of their own within five years he would quit. And he was true to his word.

We were already away on a pre-season tour to Exmouth when it happened, and the first the team knew of the upheaval was when we heard on the radio news on the team bus that Denis Dunford, who had made his fortune building from nothing a door-to-door milk delivery service, was the new chairman of Bristol Rovers.

The reorganised board immediately set out to cut the club's costs, cancelling the contracts of several of the senior players like Aiden McCaffery and Brian Williams who were on the highest wages, and giving Bobby a shoestring budget. And of course for a manager appointed by one board of directors it was unnerving to find himself working immediately for a different group.

The new chairman made his first trip away with the team in October when we went down to Bournemouth. It was another of those away day disasters as we got thrashed 6-1, and Bobby Gould couldn't wait to get the players back to Hambrook to have another of his late night inquests on the bus. His eyebrows were knitted with fury as he waited for the directors to get off the coach first before he could vent his spleen on the players. And then Denis, the most good mannered man in the world, left him utterly confused by vigorously shaking his hand and thanking him for a wonderful day out!

As the season wore on there were rumours that Rovers might leave Eastville and play instead at Bath. I don't think anybody took them seriously. When you look back now it's obvious that the club must have been losing money hand over fist. We were getting less fans per day in those days than there are season ticket holders now. But it really didn't seem that things were so bad. We enjoyed a bright start to the New Year with four successive League wins and a thrilling 3-1 victory over Leicester in the Cup in which Trevor Morgan scored two goals. A couple more wins in April made sure all fear of relegation was gone, and so we reached the final home game of the season feeling reasonably optimistic that we'd do better at Eastville next year.

Morgan was on the scoresheet again in a 1-1 draw with Chesterfield, and after the game as the crowds disappeared we were enjoying a drink and a quiet chat over what had gone right and wrong that season.

Then came the bombshell. Gordon Bennett drove up in a furniture van and told us we had to pack up everything and leave Eastville within an hour. The first reaction was disbelief. I thought he was playing a joke on us all. But the reality was spelled out that the directors had decided to tear up their £52,000-a-year lease on their historic home and pay just £22,000 to play at Twerton Park.

Needless to say we all put our shoulders to the wheel and began to clear out all the club's equipment. I had already loaded my van with the playing gear, so I helped strip the boardroom of all the furniture, trophies, and every last item that belonged to Bristol Rovers. Roy Dolling produced a crowbar from somewhere and began to remove anything that was fixed to the walls. Word was going round, and the few supporters who were still in the bars came to help too.

One thing we also took was a huge safe that was about four feet high. It was a huge, old fashioned thing – the sort of safe you'd see in a cartoon or a 1940s film. Gordon was adamant it had to go because it contained all the deeds and the records of stocks and shares that the club had owned. But nobody else could see the contents. It had to go with him. Bit by bit the furniture lorry became loaded to the roof, and it was all moved back to Hambrook to be stored. If you've ever moved house you'll know how much stuff there seems to be to find a place for. Believe me moving a football club is a hundred times harder!

I suppose it had been essential to keep it all a secret. I'm sure if people had known there would have been massive protests – and the crowd would have wanted to take bits away as souvenirs. As it was the last game at Eastville after 90 years of Bristol Rovers matches was watched by only 3,576 people.

During the summer an army of people did the jobs needed to bring Twerton Park up to some sort of standard. They painted everything that didn't move, while the supporters club set up souvenir stalls and the presidents club found a room to move into. The dressing-rooms were small, the showers creaked, the referee's room was an embarrassment, and everything would need to be improved over a period of time. I don't think that these days the move would be allowed because there are minimum standards – and rightly so.

Bob's enthusiasm was essential. Where some managers might have sulked at being forced into such a difficult position, he relished the challenge of making a success of things against the odds. Jackie Pitt was invited to go over to Bath and help out as groundsman, and the two clubs shared the cost of a £7,000 improvement scheme to the drainage.

Both clubs were determined to make the scheme work – although we weren't without our problems at boardroom level. On matchdays one of the most important jobs was to take down all the pictures of the Bath City directors which were hung on nails in the boardroom and replace them with pictures of the Bristol Rovers board. It was a vital pre-match ritual to make sure that they were all replaced. And it never caused a problem until our directors decided it would be a nice gesture to invite Bath's chairman Paul Richards and some of his board to a game. Everybody had a jolly afternoon and all was well.

All- that is – except for the fact that the next time we arrived for a home game we found the Bath City boardroom pictures were no longer on nails but had been screwed to the wall and couldn't be taken down! So we went out and bought a Rovers flag from the souvenir stall, hung that over the Bath pictures, and then put our directors on to another wall!

For a while I was doing all the catering for the boardroom, but it just got too much even for me and so the chairman's wife Joan, together with director Ron Craig's wife Anne, took over providing the buffet. I still had to take all the drinks to each match – the beers, wines and spirits. The only thing we were allowed to keep at Twerton were a few glasses. Everything else had to be brought in on the day of a game – and it was only later that we were afforded the luxury of a cupboard to keep our own drinks there all the time.

My matchday duties were getting ridiculous now. A typical Saturday of a home game began at 8am when I drove from my flat in Westbury in my yellow Suzuki van to collect the previous day's training kit from Southmead where Mrs Grinham had got it all washed from the night before. Then I'd take that back to Hambrook, before collecting the playing kit which I had to take to Bath.

I used to take more than 1,000 different items, all sorted and checked against a carefully prepared list. Once when we were at Eastville we played Doncaster Rovers who were in green and the only goalkeeper's jersey I had packed was also green. It was easy then to race up to Hambrook to get another. If you found you had forgotten something when you got to Bath you wouldn't have such a simple solution, so I became almost paranoid about making sure everything was checked and packed.

My list would include 100 of each type of stud, 24 sets of shin pads, tie-ups of different lengths, all the boots, all the balls, towels, pants, shorts, socks, shirts, warm-up tops, run-out shirts, benchwear for the subs and so on. After a while it was such a routine that nothing could go wrong, but I still worried that it would.

Once we got to Bath I would help Vi Harris and Marie Ford cut all the sandwiches for both the boardroom and the dressing-rooms.

Then make sure there were no problems with the kit downstairs. And then serve drinks in the boardroom.

So my day had begun at eight and rarely finished until maybe 10pm by which time I would just drop exhausted into bed. And people ask me why I never got married. How exactly did I have the time to go out and meet anyone?

About this time Bobby Gould decided that everybody should have their job specifications typed out so we all knew what our responsibilities were. I've still got the closely-typed list of 23 different duties, which were:

JOB SPECIFICATION

Title: Kit Manager

Responsible to: R.A. Gould – Manager

Responsible for:

1. Prepare all training kit for all professionals and apprentices from Monday to Friday
2. Take dirty training kit to laundry and collect – daily
3. Ensure apprentices have bibs, bollards and footballs ready for daily training
4. Take all training kit to venues and assemble
5. Prepare lunches for apprentices daily
6. Prepare all kit for 1st team, reserves, SEC and Parkway
7. Take all kit to Bath and assemble for 1st team and reserve matches
8. Assemble South East Counties kit for home matches at Hambrook
9. Check with Mr Bennett re: drinks for visitors room, sponsors lounge and boardroom
10. Prepare food for boardroom on match days
11. Entertain visiting Directors and guests on match days
12. Collect half-time scores for boardroom
13. Control of Public Address System for games
14. Check dressing-rooms at half-time re running bath for players at full time

15. Arrange signings of footballs and photographs for charities
16. Take kit to laundry after matches – 1st team, reserves and South East Counties
17. Return playing kit, medical kit, footballs etc to Hambrook after games
18. Collect clean laundry and return to store room
19. Check with Mr Gould re food for away matches
20. Prepare meals on coach for return journey
21. Partly cook food at home for away matches
22. Collect food from Warehouse for club's use
23. Take all damaged kit for repair

Special duties   Consult with Mr Gould re general duties daily.

Keith Valli had actually taken over my duties as the PA announcer just before we left Eastville, but it was still quite a workload, wasn't it? But somehow it all seemed to get done every week and there was still time to have a laugh with the players and listen to their woes and problems. I should mention that being a bit of a father figure to a lot of young lads who were making their way in the game was probably duty number 24 – even if it wasn't written down on the official list.

In the summer, after the shock of quitting Eastville, came another reminder of the club's financial crisis when an Extraordinary General Meeting was called to sell the Hambrook Training Ground. I still have the letter which chairman Denis Dunford sent to all shareholders explaining the need for this drastic measure, losing the piece of land which many still believed could one day be the home of a new stadium.

It sets out assets of £150,000 – the value of Hambrook at that time – and debts of £342,00. With the players we had valued optimistically at a further £150,000, it was clear the club was insolvent and on the brink of going out of business.

The new board – the chairman, Denis Dunford, and his son, Geoff, had been joined by Ron Craig, Roy Redman, Mike Ross and Vernon Stokes – got together with some of their wealthy friends to form a company which paid £250,000 for the site and then rented it back to the football club for £20,000 a year. It was a lifesaving decision for the club, but it meant we were back to the days of owning nothing.

It was obvious we were going to have to economise in many more ways, and that Bobby's gift for finding players from nowhere would be vital. He pulled out another couple of trumps before the next season even started.

In pre-season we went on a trip to France, and on the ferry back we met up with the Leeds youth team who had also been on tour. Bob found two young lads called John Scales and David Mehew feeling sorry for themselves, and discovered they had both just been told they were being released. Bobby immediately asked them both down to Bristol for trials and signed the pair of them! They both went straight into the first team as well.

Bobby also signed on a free transfer a defender called Geoff Twentyman from Preston. I had to find a hotel for him to stay in, and chose a very basic place up on Clifton Downs. I got a rollocking because I was told it was too expensive – but I stuck up for Geoff and said that if they couldn't afford to put him up they shouldn't have signed him in the first place!

Gerry Francis moved on early in the campaign, and Bobby replaced him as player-coach with the recently-signed Kenny Hibbitt. It was an inspired move and Hibbitt, who had played a record number of games for Wolves, was a superbly loyal servant to Rovers too. He worked tirelessly for Bobby Gould and then again for Gerry Francis later, and I don't think got as much credit as he deserved.

Bobby had a routine on Friday which he called POETS day. That stood for "Piss Off Early Tomorrow's Saturday". And all the pros would go home after a gentle hours training to rest for the match.

There was no rest for Bobby though. After changing he'd drive to Bath and put his wellies on and get out on the pitch helping the YTS lads, under Jackie Pitt's instruction, to try to fork away some of the water left by the natural spring in one corner of the ground which never seemed to stop pouring forth a flood.

About this time Gordon Bennett felt he could no longer take the strain of trying to work what seemed like 24 hours a day, and he left to become West Bromwich Albion secretary. A chap called Paul Britton was lined up to replace him – only he then had a big pools win and decided he could do without the long hours that went with working for the Rovers! So Bob Twyford, who had been a PR man in the police force, got the job instead.

It was a long hard season, with crowds of little more than 2,000 and results that did not much to encourage any others to make the trek from Bristol to Bath. The economy cuts were biting deeper. We cancelled pre-match stops at hotels and just pulled the bus into the roadside and ate toast. Bobby would take the players for a walk while I got the toast and jam ready. The days of steak and Dover sole at posh hotels that we had enjoyed just a few years earlier were long gone.

We negotiated for a while for the reserves to play at Forest Green in Nailsworth. They had the pokiest dressing-rooms you could imagine – barely eight feet square. And being on the top of a hill it cost us a fortune in match balls because if one was kicked out of the ground it rolled away and was never seen again. Mind you, that was a problem at Bath too where a housing estate was behind one end of the ground. When a ball got kicked over there – especially after dark – you couldn't hope to get it back. Before long the reserve and youth teams were scrapped altogether. It sounds harsh, but money had to be saved. You either cut corners or didn't have a club at all, and it generated a "backs to the wall" sort of spirit as we all pulled together to survive.

By the end of the year even Bobby's enthusiasm must have been under test. He decided to walk away from Bristol Rovers again – this time to manage Wimbledon. I suppose we'd given him an ideal training to sort out the Crazy Gang with the unorthodox Sam Hammam. And he thoroughly deserved his golden moment winning the FA Cup the very next year.

The happy-go-lucky Brough Fletcher, who didn't bother to attend the board meeting which decided to sack him. Instead he went for a drink and the club posted his notice through the door of his home.

Two of Brough Fletcher's signings for Rovers – both local boys and two of the club's best-ever servants. Harry Bamford (left) was a right-back who played the game like a centre-forward. He died tragically, in a motor-cycle accident in October 1958, after making 533 appearances for the club. Geoff Bradford (right) scored 260 goals in 523 League and Cup games for the club.

Bert Tann served Rovers as manager from 1950 to 1968. He turned a team of local players and free transfers into one of the best teams in the old Division Two after their promotion in 1953. In 1956, Rovers finished only four points adrift of promotion to the top flight.

Rovers forwards Barry Meyer, Vic Lambden, Geoff Bradford and George Petherbridge on the attack against Doncaster Rovers at Eastville in August 1953, on Rovers' return to the old Second Division.

West Ham's Dave Sexton beats Rovers' Ray Warren to the ball at Upton Park in September 1954.

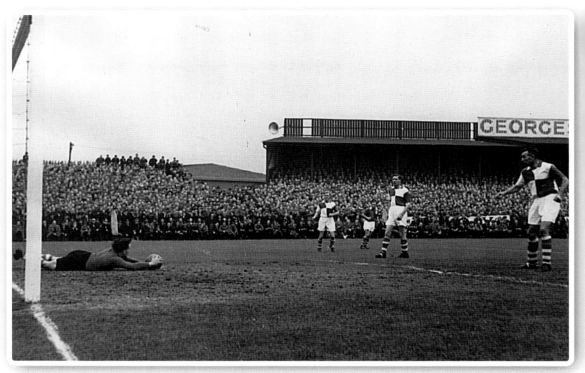

Rovers' goalkeeper Howard Radford holds the ball during the Bristol derby at Ashton Gate in October 1955.

David Ward scores against Rotherham United at Eastville in March 1956. Despite appearances, the goal was not a header.

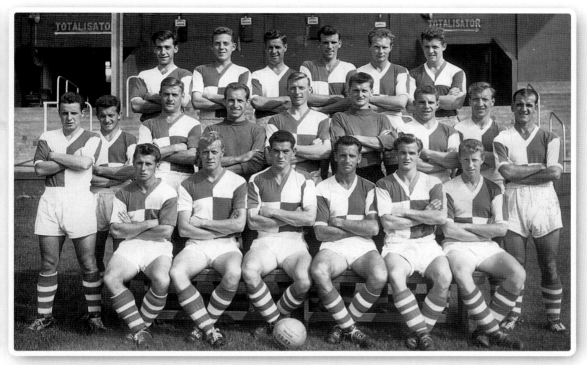

Rovers line-up in 1960-61. Back row (left to right): H. Jarman, J. Timmins, P. Sampson, A. Walker, J. Davis, A. Hall. Middle row: T. Baker, R. Mabbutt, J. Frowen, H. Radford, D. Pyle, M. Norman, D. Hillard, B. Doyle, J. Watling. Front row: G. Smith, A. Biggs, N. Sykes, G. Bradford, D. Ward, P. Hooper.

Civil Service tennis finals day in 1964. That's me on the extreme right and on the extreme left is Ron Moules, the man who introduced me to the idea of working for Bristol Rovers.

Fred Ford, the former Rovers coach who returned to Eastville as manager in 1968 and discovered players like Larry Lloyd, Frankie Prince and Wayne Jones, all of whom went on to win international honours.

Bill Dodgin was 58 when Rovers appointed him in place of Fred Ford, who had gone to Swindon Town. He stayed for three seasons and in that time Rovers enjoyed a reputation for playing attacking football.

Dream start... Don Megson replaced Bill Dodgin and saw Rovers win the Watney Cup and gain promotion to the old Division Two the following season.

Celebrations after we won the Watney Cup in 1972, beating Sheffield United 7-6 on penalties after a goalless game in normal time.

Rovers in 1974-75, back in Division Two. Back row (left to right): Frankie Prince, Ken Stephens, Peter Aitken, Trevor Jacobs, John Rudge, Middle: Tom Stanton, Stuart Taylor, Jim Eadie, Dave Staniforth, Dick Sheppard, Alan Warboys, Lindsay Parsons. Front: Bobby Campbell (trainer), Gordon Fearnley, Bruce Bannister, Don Megson (manager), Bryn Jones, Malcolm John, Colin Dobson (player-coach).

'Smash and Grab' – Bruce Bannister (left) and Alan Warboys (below). Bannister scored 91 goals in 234 League and Cup games for Rovers. Warboys, seen here in action against Manchester United, hit 62 in 162 games.

Bobby Campbell was 55 when he succeeded Don Megson as manager in November 1977. In his two years in charge he was involved in record transfer deals, both in and out of Eastville, and also produced some entertaining football and plenty of goals.

Stuart Taylor left Rovers in May 1980 after a remarkable 632 senior games for the club. Bristol-born, he was once turned down by City! Stuart captained the Rovers side which won promotion in 1973-74 by finishing runners-up in the Third Division.

A great servant… Harold Jarman, seen here in his Rovers playing days, took over from Bobby Campbell and although he was in charge for only four months, he saw the team gain enough points to get out of trouble at the foot of the Second Division. As a player Harold had made 511 League and Cup appearances and scored 145 goals.

Terry Cooper arrived at Eastville with a great playing record for Leeds and England behind him, but he couldn't delay the drop to Division Three for Rovers. Despite Rovers being in the top six, he was sacked in October 1981 after we lost 4-1 at home to Swindon. He enjoyed a much better time across the city at Ashton Gate.

Bobby Gould had two spells as Rovers boss. In his first he brought big names like Alan Ball and Mike Channon to the club on short-term contracts. In his second he had to streamline the playing staff so that Rovers could pay their debts. Bobby went to Wimbledon in 1987.

Bobby Gould's squad for his second spell as manager in 1986.

Dave Williams was a surprise choice as Rovers' player-manager after Bobby Gould left for the first time. Nevertheless, David did well and under him we had an fine home record. A bit more success away from home and we would probably have won promotion. David had a great career as a Rovers player – 400 senior games in all – and later did well at Norwich City, in whose colours he is seen here and where he was capped for Wales.

Gerry Francis, a former England captain, became manager when Bobby Gould left for a second time. Gerry had been playing for the club as player-coach and was the obvious successor to Bobby. In his time with Rovers, Gerry won us promotion and took us to Wembley.

Two great stars for Rovers but players who, sadly, we couldn't hold on to. Nigel Martyn (left) and Gary Penrice (right) both left in the autumn of 1989 for club record fees, money which Rovers just couldn't turn down. Watford paid £500,000 for Gary, while Palace spent £1 million to take Nigel to Selhurst Park.

All smiles at Wembley with Marcus Stewart and Paul Tovey, while Dennis Booth gets on with his work in the background.

On the pitch at Wembley before the Leyland Daf Final against Huddersfield, with director Ron Craig (left) and his brother-in-law, Peter Smith.

We lost at Wembley but the welcome home in Bristol, on board an open-top bus, was still a memorable occasion.

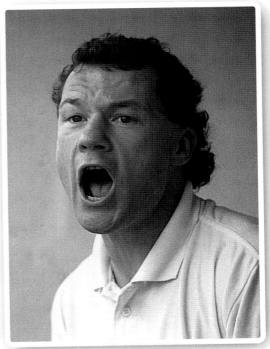

Martin Dobson commanded respect in his short time at Bristol Rovers – but he's the only former manager I served under who doesn't send me a Christmas card!

Dennis Rofe took over from Martin Dobson and was asked if he would like Malcolm Allison to help him. He could hardly say no!

Dennis Rofe with his team group, full of optimism at the start of the 1992-93 season.

Big Mal – he soon took over, telling the players that they weren't fit and couldn't kick a ball!

John Ward replaced Big Mal – and hit the place like a whirlwind. I doubt a new broom has ever tried to sweep so clean! It seemed to work OK because we found ourselves back at Wembley.

Celebrations in the Villa Park dressing-room after Malcolm Allison's side held Ron Atkinson's Aston Villa to an FA Cup draw. Big Mal – and Fat Ron as Malcolm called him – never spoke to each other once!

There aren't many trophy-winning pictures in Rovers history – but this is one of them. It was taken after we'd won the 1994 Gloucestershire Cup Final 11-10 on penalties. It was amazing and at one point managers John Ward and City's Joe Jordan suggested that they might take a kick each!

Ian Holloway. In all my years at Bristol Rovers, I don't think I ever met a player or a manager so consistently or contagiously enthusiastic as Ian.

With comedian Eddie Large at my testimonial dinner.

My testimonial match about to kick-off. Coventry City manager Phil Neal did me proud by honouring the fixture after Bobby Gould left Highfield Road.

GERRY FRANCIS

THERE can rarely have been such an obvious managerial appointment as Gerry Francis. As Bobby Gould went to Wimbledon so Francis, who was first team coach for Sam Hammam's side, was ready to step up into management. And as an ex-Rovers player himself it was obvious for him to come back to the West Country.

Not that Gerry did actually come to the West Country in the sense he never moved his home from Surrey. That was where his booming antiques business was based. But he did throw himself into the challenge of managing Rovers with both heart and soul.

I suppose he had something to prove to himself because his previous spell as a manager – some four years earlier with Exeter City – had been a huge disappointment. His team were relegated, and he had drifted around Cardiff, Swansea and Portsmouth and Wimbledon in short playing stints before Bobby Gould had taken him to Eastville and regenerated his enthusiasm.

Now he was back in the big chair – although that's probably not a good expression to describe managing Rovers at that time when we were scattered across different buildings in different locations and probably there wasn't a chair for him to sit in most of the time!

Anyway he soon learned he'd have to use as much skill and judgement selling and buying players as he did with his antiques business.

I think that John Scales had been sold to Wimbledon for £70,000 in the few days between Bobby Gould leaving and Gerry taking over, but that bit of money, however welcome, was still not going to sort out the club's overall financial problems.

Yet just like Bobby Gould, Gerry was to prove a dab hand at finding players for nothing. And the first of them was the best of the lot – probably the only England goalkeeper ever discovered by a tea lady!

It had been during the previous summer that Vi Harris, the lady who used to do the teas at the training ground, went to St Blazey in Cornwall for her holidays, along with Alwyn the chap she lived with. They wandered into the town one night and found themselves watching a game of football in which Nigel Martyn was playing as a full-back. Well the St Blazey goalkeeper got injured during the game, and Nigel took over between the sticks and played a blinder. St Blazey realised they had found something special and kept Nigel in the number-one jersey for the rest of the season. And the tea lady came back to Rovers talking about how brilliant this young lad in Cornwall had been.

She mentioned it to Bobby Gould, but unusually for him I think he forgot to pursue it. But when Gerry arrived and felt he needed competition for Tim Carter, he told Roy Dolling who coached the goalkeepers to hunt for a suitable second keeper. And Vi kept on at Roy – in between serving cups of tea – about this lad in Cornwall. She even gave him the addresses and phone number to follow up.

So Roy asked Nigel up for a trial, Gerry got involved along with Kenny Hibbitt, and they signed him straightaway. As they say the rest – given that he's now got loads of England caps and has starred for Leeds in the Champions League – is history.

Nigel was thrown straight into the first team, and did so well that even though Timmy Carter came back for a short time Gerry soon grabbed the chance to sell him to Sunderland for £50,000 and keep Nigel as his undisputed number one.

He was a tower of strength, too, standing 6ft 2ins with a massive near-15 stone frame and great big hands. And he was such a likeable man too, with no edge even as he established his reputation. He was a typical quiet, thoughtful Cornishman whose family used to travel up to watch him. They didn't miss a home match, and not many away either which is remarkable when you think they probably had three hours journey just to reach Bristol and start the away trip for real!

Nigel had only recently been married, and the club found him a place to live in Bristol above a shop in Staple Hill – and he hadn't been up here long when his wife Mandy had an accident with a plate glass door which swung and cut her leg badly. I remember Roy Dolling had to dash there from Kingswood to take her to hospital where she had lots of stitches in her leg.

Gerry was happy about settling his goalkeeper down. He was very defensive minded in the sense that he wanted a team that was solid at the back before he worried about how they would go forward. He was also a deep thinker about the game, always rubbing his chin as he watched training or matches and contemplated his next move. He also instilled great confidence to players, drumming home to them exactly what he wanted them to do. Geoff Twentyman was one who immediately began to benefit as Gerry spent ages with him drumming home the idea that he should be positive in everything he did, whether he was simply heading or kicking the ball away or more often trying to pass it with accuracy.

Roy Dolling's work – together with the efforts of old Rovers stalwarts like Joe Davis, Harold Jarman and Bobby Jones – was helping him find other players from non-League football who slowly gelled into a team. Jeff Meacham came from Trowbridge, Andy Reece from Willenhall, and Devon White from Boston United. And when he then wanted to pay a £10,000 fee to bring Ian Holloway back to the club from Brentford Gerry proved his commitment by finding the money out of his own pocket to finance the deal.

We started the season with Rob Turner up front – a big awkward striker who was very good at using his elbows. He'd probably be sent off every five minutes nowadays, but at that time strikers could still get away with a fair bit of physical stuff and Rob wasn't afraid to dish it out. He didn't intend to hurt anybody, but he was so keen to get goals he didn't care who got in the way – and just to prove there was nothing malicious in it as far as the opposition were concerned he once broke Geoff Twentyman's nose in training as well!

Turner lost his place very quickly, though. He missed the train from his Cardiff home for a match against Aldershot and Gerry put Devon White into the team for his debut. Devon took his chance, scored a goal in a 3-1 win, and poor Turner only ever started one more match before being sold to Wimbledon for £15,000 in December.

One of Tim Carter's last games, incidentally, cost us a £50 fine. He loved to wear padded shorts, and we had a black pair for away games which were the same colour as our change kit. Well we played at Notts County who were wearing black shorts as normal with their striped kit, and I went to see the referee to ask if it was okay for Tim to wear his padded pair. He told me that was no problem, so everything seemed fine. But a week later we got a letter from the League telling us we were out of order. We wrote back saying the referee had agreed – but it appeared he could be overruled after the event by his assessor sitting in the stand. So we had to cough up our fifty quid – although at least the £50,000 we got from Sunderland helped us to pay it! Nowadays goalkeepers seem to wear any combination of colours they choose irrespective of the opposition.

I don't think Gerry was too happy about that. He liked everything done just so. And he certainly made me suffer when we travelled to York on an overnight trip at the end of January and I forgot to take any footballs for training.

It didn't seem a problem when we arrived on the Friday evening to our stop at the Post House hotel, a magnificent place which overlooks the race course. Gerry took the lads out after tea for a light run and didn't want to do any football work. But when he realised we were next to a park complete with goalposts, he decided on Saturday morning that he'd like to do a little bit of work on the pattern of play.

I was panicking because we had no footballs, but Roy Dolling suggested we'd simply go to Bootham Crescent and ask to borrow some. My old saying is "I can remember a thousand things, but not a thousand and one". And it was only walking distance from the training area, so where was the problem?

Well the problem was that it started snowing very heavily, and I found myself walking back from Bootham Crescent carrying a big back of training balls, only to reach the park and find that Gerry had decided to get the boys back to the sanctuary of the hotel. So I trekked on through what had now become a snowstorm, with two or three inches already settled, and returned to find the rest of the team. Within minutes the news filtered through that the game was now off because of the weather – and like Scott of the Antarctic I got sent back out again to trek back to Bootham Crescent through the blizzard and return the balls to their rightful owners!

Another walk through the snowstorm followed to reach the hotel, and then Gerry decided we would all head back to Bristol. "Oh," he said to me. "And find us all a meal somewhere." Within 20 minutes I'd made contact with the Post House at Haydock who made us more than welcome on the way home – so all was well that ended well! It was the only time I can remember Gerry being upset with me, but it was typical of him that it was an incident soon forgotten – although I don't think we ever travelled without training balls again!

We had a tiny squad which was getting smaller because the reserve team was scrapped as another economy measure. And to add to our problems David Mehew went down with a nasty virus which kept him out for most of the season while in February Kenny Hibbitt who was so influential as both a coach and a player broke his leg during a 4-0 win against Sunderland.

That game was memorable for other reasons, because the Sunderland players were so angry at the defeat and I think a couple of refereeing decisions that they decided to smash up the dressing-room. They ripped all the ceiling tiles out above the plunge bath, and in fact were lucky because if one of the lighting tubes had fallen into the water they might have been electrocuted!

There were many protests raised, and Sunderland had to pay to repair all the damage. Somehow their bill for a new ceiling also covered the costs of replacing the old-fashioned plunge bath with smart new showers which was a great improvement.

Gerry had a fascinating style of management, almost always arriving late for training and then fining himself and paying it in cash there and then. Then when training finished he would stay out on the pitch with his coach Des Bulpin discussing some fine point of the game or another, and pinging a few balls about himself. I think it was his way of staying away from the players so he could achieve the maximum impact when matchday arrived.

He used to drive down from his Surrey home in a beautiful Saab turbo convertible, and then get me to go and refill it with petrol. Given that his home was 120 miles away it needed refilling most days! It was a wonderful car, and I used to love bowling along in it. But when you'd pull up at the lights, and people could see your head and shoulders, many a time they would shout at me: "You big headed so and so". I used to shout back: "Yes, and don't worry because I've got the money to go with it!" Then I'd drive away in that car and pick up speed as quickly as I could. That was an event every day going to fill that car!

Gerry had a thing about Saab cars. They offered him all sorts of others but he wouldn't countenance them, and eventually they got the Saab dealer to sponsor it for him. He would often bring his father down in it. He was a postman so he finished early and drove down with Gerry, and he would arrive at the training ground with his uniform still on. There was another friend of his, called Ted Sellers, who was a police inspector who came regularly too. Both of them were great company to talk to and somehow made my day. So often nowadays the art of conversation has gone out of the window.

The new directors were always looking for ways to save money, and the next one came in the summer of 1988 when we moved away from Hambrook altogether and went to the playing fields at Fry's factory in Keynsham as our training base. There were four Portakabins at the bottom of the field which would be our new home. One small one was divided as the manager's office, plus a room for all the coaches alongside. At the other end was the kitchen to do the cooking – all we could do was soup, rolls and salads for the trainees now. The next cabin was mine, with a boot room at one end and all the other kit laid out at the other. And then the last cabin belonged to the youth department. Roy Dolling insisted on displaying all the trophies he'd won with the youngsters down the years, and they probably took up more room than anybody else had. But he justified it because it was part of his "hard sell" when he had youngsters there and was convincing their parents to let them sign on. Roy actually managed to work himself a bigger section than the manager to display all his wares!

One of my jobs was to find Gerry some breakfast when he got there. He would always take time to eat it, even if he was running late as usual. Sometimes he'd even arrive from London having driven all the way with his football boots on.

For a man who had captained England and seen life at the top he had no airs or graces. He was quite happy to muck in with the rest of us in the way of life at a club where you had to make the best of what you'd got. But then he was never too proud to tell you that he had been brought up as a kid in a prefab house. And I suppose when you think of his humble beginnings, and the changes that had taken place in his life, he was entitled to enjoy his luxurious Saab!

Working at Fry's was a nightmare with the kit. We had four dressing-rooms which weren't big enough, and as much as we tried to organise things on a wet day it always left us with problems. The pitches were on a base of red clay which made everything filthy – and the goalkeepers especially were always caked in it. I used to get the goalkeepers including Nigel Martyn to go in the shower with all their kit on to wash it all off and then put it in the pile.

I would put the dirty washing in an old ashbin or plastic rubbish sacks, but I could never lift it because of the weight. Luckily in those days the YTS boys were there to help you, and I made good use of them. If you had 30 people training who had all got soaked through it made a massive problem.

They would put their dirty, wet kit in piles. All the shirts, shorts, socks, tracksuits, sweatshirts and wet tops would all go in piles in the middle of the room. Then I'd have to put them in bags, and drag them to the van. I had to take it all to a launderette in Keynsham – Spruce Launderette, it was called, where Fay and Lisa did the washing. I would park on the pavement with the front wheels so that the water would all run out of the back of the van! It used to run down the street and discolour the tarmac. Then we'd drag the washing bags into the shop which needed mopping out before they could get working on it.

Somehow still I could invariably take it all there at four in the afternoon following a double session of training, and come back at 7.30am the next morning and it would all be perfect. People wondered why I started so early – but if I left my flat in Westbury at seven I could get across town to get the washing in 20 minutes. If I waited just half an hour later to leave home the journey took 90 minutes. So it was much easier to rise with the larks, then get the gear across to Fry's and I still had time to put it all out on hangers in the individual dressing-rooms ready for when the lads reported for their day's training.

All the gear was individually numbered, of course, which created silly little jobs like pairing up 36 pairs of socks! You had to put all the kits together on hangers with a towel and a pair of pants. When I write it all down now I wonder how I did it all, but at the time it was just a simple daily routine – even if it was a mammoth task.

The next step forward was to give the physio a room in the lower basement of the building at Fry's. Roy Dolling and I brought all the weights over from Hambrook to get it equipped out, and by our standards we'd created a luxury facility to help get the injured players fit again. Outside contractors did assemble the weight training gear which was a specialist job – but we did the hardest part by carrying it over to Fry's in the first place.

None of it was ideal. At Easter time they would clear everybody out of the factory, close it down for the long weekend, and fumigate the whole area. When you are making mountains of chocolate it's essential to keep the highest hygiene standards, after all. For Roy and I, though, it meant a massive task clearing everything away from the training ground ready for the games at the weekend, and for more training sessions at Keynsham Town's ground. If you forgot so much as a pair of boots you were not allowed back on site to collect them. Security was that strict.

Yet Gerry's down to earth attitude made the best of the difficulties, and slowly a "backs against the wall" spirit grew which was reflected in the team's performances. Gary Penrice's successful conversion to a striker brought him 20 goals in the 1988-89 season and the average gate went up over the 5,000 mark. We finished the season, unbelievably, reaching the play-offs and after thrashing Fulham 5-0 on aggregate hopes were high that the impossible could be achieved and we'd gain promotion.

The final that year was over two legs rather than at Wembley – but after drawing 1-1 at home to Port Vale we lost by the only goal in the second game. John Rudge, Vale's manager and a popular Bristol Rovers old boy, had done his homework and knew exactly how to stop our team.

Even so, as we got over that disappointment there was a growing feeling that the group of lads we'd put together had plenty of promise. And after our summer break we were looking forward to the new campaign.

CHAMPIONS – AND A TRIP TO WEMBLEY

BY the start of the next season Gerry knew his best team and he wasn't going to change it. We were unchanged for the first ten games, and the confidence grew. Before long we were third, then second, and then incredibly a 4-2 home win over Northampton took us top of the table.

Gerry had his team built now around a strong defence with a group of powerful characters. There was fiery Ian Alexander at right-back, a Scot who would argue with anyone and kick his granny if required. Vaughan Jones was becoming an inspirational captain at left-back. But most important was the central pairing of Geoff Twentyman and Steve Yates.

It's amazing to think that Yates had almost been let go by the club a couple of years earlier when the reserve team was scrapped. I think he'd been told he would be released before the Presidents Club members who had watched him emerge through the youth teams offered to pay his wages. They wanted a Bristol boy to play for Bristol Rovers, and were rewarded as he established himself superbly in the first team.

The other Bristol boy who was the crowd's biggest favourite was

Ian Holloway, a livewire little midfield dynamo. Although he was to play an even bigger role in the club's history a few years later.

But most important of all, it seemed, was goalkeeper Nigel Martyn who by now was an England under-21 international and attracting scouts from all over the country. He went through six matches without conceding a goal, and it was obvious that no ambitious club would sell him, would they?

When Gary Penrice went to Watford in October for £500,000 that was a blow. We had lost our goalscorer, but at least it seemed to us that the money worries would be eased a bit and we could hang on to Nigel. But then just a month later came a £1m offer from Ron Noades, the chairman of Crystal Palace. And the board decided that this was simply too good to turn down.

To be honest we felt it was crazy. Why were we letting our best players go just when we had a chance of winning something? Of course we understood that you couldn't stand in Nigel's way, but the timing seemed all wrong. Just as there had once been criticism of the "no buy, no sell" ethos, now people were angry that we were taking money for our best players.

While Nigel went to Selhurst Park for the record fee ever paid for a goalkeeper, we got Palace's reserve Brian Parkin to take his place on a free transfer. It seemed a huge let down – but Rovers fans were to find out that they weren't any worse off at all.

Brian took on the challenge of replacing Nigel with great confidence and put together his own sequence of clean sheets.

In fact it was probably Brian who turned the tide back in our favour after a disappointing spell of results through December and January when we dropped out of the automatic promotion places. He performed heroics with saves in a penalty shoot-out at Brentford in the Leyland Daf Cup, and reaching the regional semi-finals seemed to give all the lads a huge boost to their confidence.

The atmosphere on away trips was brilliant now. We had so many characters in the side. And they had their fun at my expense when we played a night match at Leyton Orient.

We stopped at the Swallow Hotel in Waltham Abbey for our pre-match meal, but left in plenty of time to reach the ground. We got on to the M25, and the coach driver prepared to turn back off again at the next exit.

That was where Geoff Dunford became map reader, and insisted that we needed to go one more junction down. The driver, naturally did as he was told by a senior director. But when we then followed his route we found ourselves coming into London down a completely different, and congested, set of roads with the rush hour traffic in full swing.

It was getting later and later. At seven o'clock we stopped the coach and got all the gear off so the players could get changed on board, ready to run out when they reached Brisbane Road. But we were still quite a distance from the ground, and as the coach got going again I rang on a mobile phone – still quite a novelty invention – to make contact with Leyton Orient's officials and ask for advice.

A police inspector came on the other end of the phone.

"Where are you?" he said.

Without thinking I answered: "I'm in the middle of the coach next to the tea machine."

The voice on the other end began to sound exasperated: "No, where is the coach?"

I answered again: "We're going over a zebra crossing, we have the Co-op on the right and an off-licence on the left."

Honestly, I think Benny Hill would have been proud of the script! The conversation continued in similar vein for a few more questions and answers, with by now the lads listening in and in hysterics of laughter. Eventually I handed the phone to the coach driver, who got the best instructions on how to get through the traffic, and we finally pulled up at Brisbane Road just 20 minutes before kick-off. Everyone on the coach helped take all the gear into the dressing-room and the lads, all fully changed, dashed off to head on to the pitch for their warm-up. But when I got off the coach the police inspector was stood there waiting to talk to me, demanding to know: "Who's the comedian?"

Happily he saw the funny side of it all. And although we got fined for failing to put the team sheet in at the correct time, it still all had a happy ending because we won 2-0!

The confidence was growing all the time. The team were getting to know each other, and they used to socialise together too. Vaughan Jones was not only captain but social secretary, and he organised everything. Gerry encouraged that, and gave the boys a kitty whenever they had won to finance their nights out. His England background made him wealthier than the rest of the boys by far, and he wasn't afraid to put his money where his mouth was. His view was that if the team gave him everything they had, he would give them everything he had.

Mind you, if we didn't win it wasn't such an easy life for them. Returning from an away game if we'd lost he would take every player in turn to the back of the coach and talk them through what had gone right and wrong. And he'd also play an Al Jolson tape on the bus if we'd been beaten. Gerry loved all those old songs, although everybody else hated them. So if we'd lost the sounds of *Mammy* would act as a punishment. No wonder we only got beaten five times all season!

Through the back end of the campaign we put together an incredible roll, winning eight games out of ten to climb back into second place. The only down side was that whatever we seemed to do, Bristol City were doing even better to stay on top.

In the middle of that run came the night when we secured a place at Wembley for the first time in the club's history. It may only have been the Leyland Daf Cup, but it might just as well have been the European Cup for how elated we were. We had to play Notts County in the semi-final, and battled brilliantly at Meadow Lane to hang on to a 1-0 lead from the first leg. County thought they had scored in the final minutes – and to be honest it probably was a good goal but referee Brian Hill disallowed it for a push because one of our players had been pushed out of the way to create the chance.

It was a first class decision for us – but County's players went bonkers – especially former Rovers player Nicky Platnauer who had to be restrained by Geoff Twentyman from assaulting the ref. But

Brian stuck to his decision, and the final whistle blew seconds later. We ran to celebrate with our supporters leaving County and their manager Neil Warnock to carry on their feud with the ref as they left the pitch.

The whole season came to be settled on 2 May, when City were the visitors to Twerton Park. And on a never to be forgotten night two goals from Devon White and an Ian Holloway penalty gave us an amazing 3-0 win which confirmed our promotion and took us top of the table. It was a contrast for me to the first time Rovers had got promotion, all those years before under Bert Tann. Then I had been on the microphone and watching the game. This time I was so busy with my backroom duties that I hardly saw a ball kicked – although I've watched the game a good few times on video since!

Nevertheless I enjoyed the celebrations which went on long into the night. And three days later hordes of Rovers fans were celebrating again as another 3-0 win at Blackpool meant we were not only up but up as champions, a really great achievement.

So it was off to Wembley, and we enjoyed a fortnight's rest and recuperation – together with some hard work on the training ground – before heading on Friday to our luxury hotel base for the big game.

With Gerry's England background he selected Burnham Beeches as our hotel. That's where the England team stayed all the time they were playing at Wembley, and the luxury has to be seen to be believed.

We had our evening meal, and decided to go for a walk around the grounds on what was a wonderful, fine May evening. But I fell for a silly one, because there's a huge lake in the middle of the grounds and at Gerry's suggestion I went and sat in one of the boats. Suddenly Gerry and director Ron Craig pulled the two oars out, and pushed the little boat adrift to send me floating to the middle of the water. They left me out there for fully 40 minutes – it seemed like hours – before coming out to rescue me so we could all return for a nightcap and enjoy a very happy end to the evening.

Next day we had breakfast and a leisurely pre-match meal before leaving for Wembley, and a police escort met us a few miles from the stadium. You can't imagine how it feels, after years of heading almost unnoticed into tiny stadiums around the country, to suddenly be driving up Wembley way with 30,000 cheering fans all around you. I seemed to have a lump in my throat all day with all the tension and excitement.

The coach drove up to the big entrance to the tunnel and the Wembley dressing-rooms, and we got out to find our first defeat of the day. Gerry had tossed a coin for choice of dressing-room beforehand, and won. Naturally, with all his wonderful memories from his international days as an England captain, he'd chosen the home room. But Tranmere's coach was already at the ground. And Tranmere's kit had already been laid out in the home changing room. Gerry went to find their manager John King, who absolutely refused to move. So we found ourselves having to be the away team.

Not that we were really complaining, because the luxury – compared to the stadiums we were used to – had to be seen to be believed. Everything was finished in beautiful leather, there was a huge plunge bath with another 15 or more showers, and three stewards waiting to help me put all the kit out. I couldn't help thinking of the contrast to places like Bury where the rooms were so tiny you could barely fit in a five-a-side team or even get your kit boxes through the doors, and had to set up the physio's table in the showers!

The players – who were dressed up to the nines in their Wembley outfit with club blazers and flannels – went out to take a look around while I got on with my jobs getting the kit all ready. And then it was my turn to walk up that long tunnel and emerge into the sunlight on to what was the most famous playing surface in the world. The grass was like a billiard table, like velvet, and the groundsman explained to me how it was cut four times every day to keep it in such perfect condition. I thought of Bobby Gould when he was dashing off after training on Fridays to put his wellies on and help fork the surface water off the mud at Twerton. I bet none of the England managers ever had to do that chore at Wembley before a game could take place!

I walked round the perimeter of the pitch, and at one end there came washing over me the most amazing sound. Some 30,000 Bristol

Rovers fans all chanting: "There's only one Ray Kendall". I felt very emotional, very proud, very exhilarated.

During the build-up to the trip I had spoken to somebody at Millwall who had told me how quickly time would go on your big Wembley day out. He wasn't wrong. It flew by, and before we knew it the time had arrived for the teams to go out. I still had another job to take care of, though. Gerry was leading the team out wearing the same posh blazer that was the players' uniform for the day – but he wasn't too happy about that.

He was a man of superstitions, and during matches that season had taken to wearing a buff-coloured siren suit with two zips that go the length of the body. Well as soon as the teams had finished lining up we had to dash off under the staircase and find somewhere for Gerry to take off all the clothes he had been wearing and put on this siren suit again. I sorted somebody to take his clothes back to the changing room, and we settled down for the game.

That's where the great day out began to hit the buffers, because Tranmere took the lead, and although Devon White gave us a marvellous moment with an equaliser early in the second half, Jim Steel headed the winning goal for Tranmere not long from the end. Gerry was furious with referee Vic Callow who he felt should have given us a penalty when big Devon White was brought down. He'd had a row with the same referee when we had lost at Notts County in the League a few weeks earlier, and was convinced this was how the official had got his own back.

But at the end of it we still had to accept defeat, and we still had more than 30,000 Rovers fans cheering the team for their exploits across a wonderful season. We headed up into the West End for a banquet to celebrate our successes, and walked into sumptuous luxury in a hotel near Trafalgar Square. There was another neat twist to come – somebody had taken the decision to save a few pounds by bringing our own wine to the hotel, and we unloaded several crates of fine wine and champagne into the banqueting hall. A nice idea – except the hotel charged us corkage and we ended up paying more than we would have done if we'd simply ordered theirs!

We came back late to Bristol the same night, and then had a bus tour around the town a few days after that. That was a wonderful experience, leaving from Fry's and driving through the Rovers heartland areas of Longwell Green, Warmley, Bitton, Kingswood and Hanham, on down to Easton and finally ending up in the car park at the Tesco supermarket which was now sited at one end of Eastville Stadium.

It was quite a contrast to be at Tesco when you think that Don Megsan's promotion celebrations had been in the splendour of the Council House. But the lads signed autographs by the hundred, and lapped up the site of thousands of people with their scarves and banners enjoying the end of a magnificent season.

We rounded up the campaign by going together to Majorca for a holiday, where the players and staff all week took the chance to wind down after a long, hard but successful season. We flew from Bristol, and the journey got held up because they gave us the full celebrity treatment. We were treated to drinks in the VIP departure lounge and given a great end of season send-off to our destination.

It was a lovely summer – but before long we were back in training and facing the task of keeping a club with no ground of its own, and no training ground of its own either, afloat in the Second Division. There was yet another crisis still to come.

In the middle of September we played at home to Hull, and I can remember we had to leave early from Bath because they had a wedding reception on in the evening at Twerton and wanted us to clear out as early as possible. At the end of another 12-hour day I headed home after putting everything away, and flopped exhausted into bed. The next morning I woke to the news on the radio that somebody had set fire to the boardroom at Twerton Park.

I set off to Bath to find out the damage, and got there to discover that it was far more than just the boardroom. Parts of the back of the stand had also been burned down and all the facilities with it. Some seating, the dressing-rooms and sponsors lounges were completely gutted with damage costing more than half a million pounds.

The story went that some Bristol City fans on their way back from a defeat at West Brom had decided to do a detour and set the ground of their rivals on fire. It was even reported that they had been arrested, but I don't know if any charges were ever brought.

Decisions had to be taken, and the directors contemplated sharing even further afield at Swindon. Or even the dreaded prospect of moving into Ashton Gate! But they voted to stay at Bath, and the job began of patching up the facilities to make it viable. Bob Twyford the secretary organised two Portkabins on top of each other, and Roy Dolling created a bar at one end of the top one to use as a boardroom. The lower one became the guest room for sponsors. It wasn't exactly luxurious. We had to use a hosepipe that ran some 150 yards from the pitch to provide running water as the only way to wash glasses.

But typically of Bristol Rovers down the years we made it work, and although it was a battle getting all the stuff up the stairs out in the open air to reach the boardroom we survived like that for a year before the main stand was rebuilt. There was temporary seating installed, and a new changing area although it was still no larger than before the fire.

On the field the combination of Carl Saunders and Devon White produced enough goals to keep us up very comfortably. After a shaky start we never so much as even flirted with relegation and Gerry picked the same 11 players week in and week out. Carl showed magnificent character to get 16 League goals. He'd suffered a horrible personal tragedy when his girlfriend's car broke down on her way to London. She stopped on the side of the motorway, only for somebody to plough into the back of the car and leave her fatally injured.

I suppose it was inevitable that after so much success, somebody would entice Gerry away to bigger and better things. At the end of the season he announced he was moving on to take over Queen's Park Rangers as they prepared to go into the top flight. It was a sad day for us to say goodbye, and I had a lump in my throat when he presented me and all the staff with a tankard. I still have mine, inscribed with "Well done Ray, thanks for four great years", among my proudest possessions. We had got so used to his routine and everybody knew what to expect. Instead a year of turbulence and chaos was to come.

MARTIN DOBSON AND DENNIS ROFE

IT was never going to be easy replacing somebody as successful as Gerry. And the directors went through a long process with many interviews as they searched for the answer.

I think every previous time when a managerial vacancy had occurred at Rovers there had always been a fairly obvious contender. There was nearly always somebody who had been at the club as a player-coach, or around in a more senior coaching role, who was about right to step up. This time we were going to have to go for an outsider. So it was that Martin Dobson emerged through the interview process to get the job.

Martin had been a superb player with Burnley and Everton through more than 600 League games at the top level, and had then won promotion from the Fourth Division to the Third with Bury. He was 43 years old so still young and ambitious, and had done well again managing in non-League football with Northwich Victoria. He said all the right things to the board, and they decided that here was the man to not only keep us in Division Two but start to take aim for the First Division. With plans to create a Premier League being widely discussed, it was a time to be as ambitious as possible.

Martin started work at the beginning of July with Dennis Rofe appointed as his number two, and he brought Tony Gill from Manchester United to coach the youngsters at the club. That was also a good move because Tony had been in Manchester United's youth set-up as the likes of David Beckham and Gary Neville were beginning to emerge – although both were unknown 16-year-olds in 1991 – and could bring some extra quality to help our own few YTS boys to develop. Tony had suffered a terrible broken leg which had finished his own playing career prematurely, but his experience of such quality coaching had made him eager to learn himself.

So the theory of it all was excellent. But in practice it was a nightmare!

Martin's first big change was to tell all the players that from now on they had to wash their own training kit every day. That wasn't a bad idea from my perspective because I was struggling a bit to keep up with all the work. But it didn't go down so well with most of the players who were used to having everything they wanted laid out for them every morning without ever needing to think about it.

His other big idea was to start training with a whistle. If we were due to begin work at 9.30 am, then at 9.30 sharp he would give a shrill blast on his whistle and training would begin. When he was ready to stop the whistle would blast again, and training was over. Everything was done to the whistle. The joke quickly began to go among the lads that we were training on the playing fields surrounding the Fry's chocolate factory, and were having to "clock in" and "clock out" to the sound of a hooter the same as the workers on the production line.

When the season began he went out and spent a club record fee of £130,000 on Justin Skinner from Queen's Park Rangers to beef up the midfield, and paid a further £40,000 for the experience of Steve Cross from Derby.

But the lads were more concerned about another unusual twist to Martin's management style. Never once did he travel to away games on the team coach. Dennis Rofe would be in charge of the group on the bus, while Martin made the journey in his own car with his wife for company. He didn't even meet up and go on the bus from the hotel if we stopped for a pre-match meal. He would just walk into the dressing -room as kick-off approached and start taking charge from there. And sadly, while he spoke sense as he went around each individual telling them what he expected from them, you could see that the respect of the players for him was slipping away.

People say that players today have changed from the days of the 1950s, and to a certain extent that is true. I think they are more in the game for themselves nowadays, when certainly the older ones were more committed to the idea of supporting the club. But the same basic principle has always held true – which is that you need not just good players but a good team spirit to be successful. The two go together.

At Rovers we always had that. The strength of the team in the great Bert Tann days of the 1950s was that they did everything together. They were mostly local lads and they stuck up for each other on and off the pitch. Gerry had built the same sort of spirit among his group of players, and suddenly it was being eroded.

Among the staff we tried to tell Martin Dobson what was happening, and I think we tried to help him. He commanded a good deal of respect from us because of both his playing pedigree and the ability he still had out on the training field.

But there was a group within the dressing-room who were losing that respect. Players like Ian Alexander, Vaughan Jones and Geoff Twentyman were very close friends away from the training ground – and players talk to each other. I think they were grumbling about how things had changed, and the new manager simply wasn't what they were used to. Suddenly that created a lack of effort in everything that happened, and the spirit at the training ground became as low as I had ever known it.

Ironically Martin, for all that he travelled on his own to away games, was probably spending more time around the club than Gerry ever did. Gerry's style had been to come and go every couple of days and try to have maximum impact. But Martin was an extremely quiet man and just didn't have the same force of personality to gain everybody's respect.

Oddly enough some of the training and coaching exercises he put on were a revelation. There was no doubt he was a quality coach and had learned from his time at both Burnley and Everton and with England. But by the time he'd blown his whistle to start it he'd already lost the backing of the lads and it wouldn't have made much difference what he did.

All the grumbling was not surprisingly reflected in the results. After starting the campaign with two draws at home to Ipswich and away to Tranmere we had lost five League games on the trot. We did beat Oxford at home, but four days later lost 3-1 to Bristol City at Twerton Park in the League Cup. The signs were not good – and then came an away trip to Brighton.

The team travelled overnight to prepare properly because it was a long, awkward journey. Martin drove down the next day with his wife and went straight to the ground to meet us again.

We lost 3-1, and I think that was the final straw for Rovers' directors who decided they had to face the fact they'd chosen the wrong man. Martin was politely told his spell as manager of Bristol Rovers was over after less than four months. And uniquely among all the bosses I have worked for I have never seen or heard from him since. I still send him a Christmas card every year – but there's never been any hint of a reply. With the prospect of starting a management search from scratch, the directors asked Dennis Rofe to stand in as caretaker. And he immediately wrote the perfect job application for himself by masterminding a 4-2 win at Ashton Gate in the second leg that took us on a Cup run!

You couldn't believe how quickly the mood of a club could change. The whistle at the start of training went straight out of the window! And while he had his own code of discipline, Dennis made everything far more relaxed. Steve Cross was promoted to be first team coach, and not only the mood improved but the results got better too.

By the time Christmas came we had beaten Bristol City again to get out of the relegation zone, and then thumped Plymouth 5-0 with Carl Saunders hitting four goals to go into the fourth round of the FA Cup.

We weren't without our problems. But at least they were the sort of physical crises that Rovers have always fought against. We'd done fire twice at Eastville and Twerton, and now it was flood! One day there was torrential rain out at Fry's, and the pitches at the bottom of the field were completely flooded. I got called out by the factory security guards at around 2.30am with torrential rain still hammering down, and the warning that the water was just about to burst through the Portakabin kit store room door. In the darkness Roy Dolling and I had to lift everything up and pile it on tables and chairs while the water flooded in. When we returned next morning in daylight it was an even bigger mess.

For several weeks afterwards we did all our training at Keynsham Town while the floods at Fry's slowly went down and the grass pitches re-emerged. I was beginning to wonder if I should swop my little van for an ark!

We were dried out by the time February arrived, and everything was in gear for the visit of Liverpool, managed by Graeme Souness. They had won five games out of five in January, scoring 12 goals in the process, and Souness was Manager of the Month.

We had a capacity crowd of nearly 9,500 squeezed into Twerton Park, and all the arrangements carefully planned to make sure the day was a success.

Before the game we entertained all their dignitaries and directors, and they were charming people. When it kicked off we had, as requested, arranged a seat in the directors box for Mr Souness to watch the game from, just next to the gangway so he could easily get in and out to take instructions to the bench.

Well that was fine, except that across the other side of the gangway Bob Twyford had allocated a seat to a city councillor. And this fellow was extremely vocal – particularly in his criticism of one or two of Liverpool's signings.

The game was exciting. Dean Saunders put Liverpool in front with an excellent goal, and then upset everybody by losing his temper and smacking Ian Alexander in the face with his elbow. Saunders got away with that challenge because the referee didn't spot it – although he was later in trouble on TV evidence. In any case I'm not sure I blame him too much because "Jock", as we knew him, would aggravate anybody for a pastime and had probably taken things a bit too far with an old pro!

As the second half went on Rovers got more and more into the game, and thoroughly deserved to go in front when our own Saunders – Carl – smashed a fantastic equaliser.

Well as we pressed to create an upset, and Liverpool defended more and more doggedly, the city councillor was hurling more and more abuse at Liverpool's manager. We sat there concentrating on the game without realising what was happening – and then suddenly Souness's patience snapped and he leaped across the aisle and angrily grabbed the councillor by the lapels! Luckily Bob Twyford spotted the incident just in time and intervened before getting two stewards to escort the councillor away from his seat!

Liverpool held on and took us to a replay – and so we looked forward to a special day out at Anfield. Dennis got permission for us to travel overnight – a rare luxury for a Saturday game never mind a midweek trip – and the whole club seemed to be involved in the party that went north to have a whale of a time.

In the afternoon Roy Dolling and I took the kit over to Anfield to get it all laid out. To prepare a dressing-room properly takes time, and it's not easy to do with all the lads there, so whenever its possible you take the chance to go early and get everything sorted out well in advance.

Once there we were met by Phil Thompson and Ronnie Moran, who provided a mug of tea and then took us on an Anfield tour. We saw the famous entrance to the tunnel, with its imposing sign saying: "This is Anfield, home of Liverpool FC." And we also did a tour of the trophy room, where every manager has his own showcase detailing the achievements of his era. We went through the wonderful story, looking at the silverware collected by first Bill Shankly, then Bob Paisley, Joe Fagan and Kenny Dalglish. And Thompson took enormous pride in showing us around. I'm not surprised that Gerard Houllier uses him now to retain the old Liverpool spirit among his more modern French ideas. We stayed with him so long that afternoon that we were late back to the hotel and missed our pre-match meal!

If the afternoon wasn't already memorable enough, I then had a walk around the pitch before the game. And just like at Wembley two years earlier I was in tears hearing 7,500 Bristolians chanting: "There's only one Ray Kendall".

The atmosphere in the dressing-room was magic, as Dennis calmed everybody down and brought their focus on to the game and the jobs they had to do. And for 45 glorious minutes everything went our way with Carl Saunders scoring again to put us in front at half-time. We needed to hold on to that advantage for a while to turn the crowd against them – but just five minutes after the interval Steve McManaman got an equaliser and then Dean Saunders again got the winner. Souness, who had definitely been riled to a fury by that councillor, had the last laugh. And he laughed longest too because Liverpool went on to win the FA Cup that year.

As for the councillor? Well he completed an unfortunate double of Liverpool legends a month later when Blackburn came to play at Twerton. He was sat in the same seat, and just opposite the aisle, again, was the visiting manager – Kenny Dalglish.

Our troublesome councillor spent much of the game pointing out what a waste of money it had been for Mr Dalglish to spend £1m on Roy Wegerle who was making his debut. And as Rovers put together a 3-0 win Dalglish, just like his old Anfield and Scotland team mate a few weeks earlier, lost his temper and pinned the city councillor to his seat! Again Bob Twyford sent for the stewards – and on Monday our poor secretary got an almighty rollocking for letting it happen so soon after the previous incident. Suffice to say that the City Councillor was moved to a seat at the back – and a long way from the gangway – after that!

The experience of going to Anfield obviously did the players good, because we went through the final 14 games of the season losing only three times. One of those games was at Cambridge where their manager John Beck was up to all sorts of tricks and we were hammered 6-1. Every time the ball went out for a throw one of their YTS lads would dry it on a towel, and then the player who was hurling it in would rub his hands on the grit track. It meant as a defender rose to head the ball away he'd get grit in his face and eye, and we didn't stand up to that trial too well. A big striker called John Taylor scored their sixth goal – and a few weeks later Dennis signed him in a swop deal for Devon White that also earned us an extra £100,000 fee.

Taylor got eight goals in as many games, and so despite all the turmoil at the start of the season we finished up 13th – the same as a year earlier. Rofe, who had taken over a team with only five points from nine games, had done brilliantly and the spirit that was so special to Rovers was back again with everybody working as one.

BIG MAL – AND FAT RON!

WE might have all come back with high hopes that summer of 1992 as pre-season training got under way – but they were completely unfulfilled. I've long ago given up trying to forecast the results of a season by how things go during the preparations. It's the hardest part of any campaign as you work and run to get everybody fit. You can be brilliant or useless in friendly games, and can simply never tell how things will turn out when the season starts for real.

As Rofe – together with his number two Steve Cross – worked the lads through their running and their warm-up games there didn't appear to be any problems. But when the season got under way we started to struggle.

Five defeats in six League games was the worst possible start. And then a place in the Anglo-Italian Cup competition which could have been a morale booster turned out to be the complete opposite. We drew at West Ham and beat Southend, only to be knocked out on the toss of a coin before the chance of any away trips came round. Having packed up what seemed like the entire club at one time or another to travel to almost every part of England, I'd been quite looking forward to the challenge of playing in Europe too!

Slowly the results got worse and worse, and the directors were not surprisingly beginning to feel the need to take some action.

That was when our chairman Denis Dunford settled down at home to watch a TV programme and saw Malcolm Allison taking some schoolkids in a coaching session. Here was a man who was widely recognised as one of the game's top football brains, and the chairman made the suggestion to the other directors to get him involved. They felt Dennis Rofe was a good manager – but maybe he could do with some help and a little variety with the actual coaching of the team.

You couldn't knock Allison's pedigree, after all. In his time he had enjoyed a flamboyant spell of success with Manchester City and had the hugest profile. Everybody knew of Big Mal, and if he was 65 years old did it matter if he could bring some experience to the training ground?

Dennis Rofe was asked if he'd like some help, and while he might not have been too keen he could hardly turn down the opportunity to learn from a legend, could he? I think he felt that Allison would come in and offer some advice for a week or so and then quietly slip away.

First impressions helped reinforce that idea. Malcolm shuffled in like an old man, and spoke quietly. His hair was white, and wearing his big raincoat he could look like an old man. But when he stripped off for training you realised he was still a powerful figure. And his personality was even more powerful. I think we had all reckoned without his massive enthusiasm for the game. He was still known as Big Mal, and it wasn't hard to see why. Within a matter of days he'd set out some radical changes that he wanted made, and he just completely took the place over. He said the players weren't fit enough, they couldn't kick the ball properly, the training was wrong, and so on.

So we became the first club to do pre-season training in November. On Monday, Tuesday and Thursday the team were taken off to Bath University to be put through a staggering series of workouts by Jed Rodey who was Bath Rugby club's fitness trainer.

That in itself was an event, for the club to be spending money on providing those sort of quality facilities. It was a sign that the board were willing to spend to keep their Second Division status. Another more obvious sign was when they paid a club record £370,000 to sign Andy Tillson from Grimsby, and then another £100,000 to bring Gary Waddock from Swindon. A further £250,000 went on Justin Channing from Queen's Park Rangers. The club's finances were being pushed to the limits, and the players were being pushed just as far as they finished every day feeling absolutely knackered.

I remember them being put to work on a huge set of 70 steps on one side of the University campus, having to sprint up them one step at a time, then two at a time, and then three.

The lads weren't so keen – especially because they were having to start work so early. But that was because Allison was also still working for Sky TV. Either Roy Dolling or myself had to drive him every day to Bath Station to catch the 10.15 to London so he could reach the studios in time to make his appearances for the fledgling Sports station.

For a man who already was suffering through having only one lung, Allison was unbelievable in his energy and his zest for life. He took us all on a trip to North Devon to try to build some team spirit, and I can still picture him puffing on a big cigar, sipping champagne and wearing that giant Fedora hat that he'd made his trademark.

His training and coaching methods were certainly unorthodox. One day he brought along two weighted, heavy leather balls the size of bowling green balls. The lads had to take turns at throwing them in the air and then catching them on the instep – and most of them simply couldn't do it. Malcolm could, incidentally – but then he had been a great player in his time. I remember watching the West Ham side of the 1950s at Eastville with John Bond, Ernie Gregory and Noel Cantwell, and Allison was a superb player.

Big Mal also had his ideas on who in the squad could play and who couldn't. He loved the younger players, and Marcus Browning in particular he praised to the nines while some of the older pros got severe treatment. He blew out Geoff Twentyman completely and demanded more and more say in picking the team.

The next surprise came when Roy Dolling and I were asked to go to Bristol airport to collect our new fitness expert. His name was Lennie Heppel, he was a tiny little man who looked very fit but was 70 years old, and as we drove back into town we started talking to him.

He was a jitterbug champion and a dance expert, he explained. And the next day we began to see how he worked. His aim was to improve co-ordination, and he took over training after Malcolm's early morning stint had finished and he'd caught the train to London. Lennie set out a long row of cones at a sports centre hall in Keynsham, and then had the players running in and out of them bending first to the left and then the right while trying to touch the opposite cone to their natural line of movement. It sounds complicated – and it was. Many of the lads simply couldn't do it, but their orders were to stay there all day until they finally got it right. In his time Lennie had worked for Newcastle, Sunderland, Manchester City in Malcolm's heyday, for Manchester United and for both Merseyside clubs so he clearly knew what he was doing. It was just that the players at Bristol Rovers weren't so sure!

It was obvious by now that Malcolm and Dennis Rofe would never get on together. The atmosphere between them got worse, and it ended up in a massive row in the middle of the training ground. Dennis went off to the board to insist that either he was the manager or he wasn't. And the board made a simple decision. He wasn't.

But as November became December, Allison's fitness regime was paying huge dividends and the results suddenly perked up. We drew at Peterborough, beat Leicester and Luton, and then hammered Bristol City 4-0 to get out of the relegation zone. Allison was getting loads of publicity and loving it, and in four weeks Bristol Rovers had never had so much national attention. When we then drew Aston Villa at home in the FA Cup, it exploded.

Villa were managed by Ron Atkinson. Big Ron. Another larger than life media character who always attracted headlines.

I personally thought Atkinson was a smashing man. I'd encountered him years earlier when we had stopped for a pre-match meal at the Post House in Newcastle-under-Lyme and Manchester United were also there. It was during Bobby Gould's time, and we were playing at Port Vale while United were on their way to West Bromwich Albion.

While Gouldy had been doing the team talk in the hotel I had slipped out to the coach to begin all my preparation work, and Atkinson – who stayed away from his players as a management ploy during the build-up to games – had invited himself on to our coach and started talking to me. I've never seen anybody with so much jewellery. He had a heavy bracelet on both wrists, a gold watch, rings everywhere it seemed except through his nose. But behind all that show he was a charming man who was genuinely interested in the amount of work I had to do to keep a small club on the road. In fact when Bobby Gould got on to the coach Big Ron told him that United needed somebody like me and asked what the transfer fee was! Gouldy just told him that even though United had just paid £1.5million for Bryan Robson they definitely couldn't afford me, and that was the end of the matter! So my big move to Manchester United came and went in seconds!

Anyway Allison clearly wasn't such a fully paid-up member of the Ron Atkinson fan club. And as the big Cup tie approached he gave an interview to the national newspapers which included the memorable quote: "I used to think he was Big Ron, but I only call him Fat Ron now."

The word from Villa Park was that Atkinson was furious. He stayed away from making any public reply, but Allison had set out to wind him up and had clearly succeeded. When the day of the game came Villa's manager did pop in to wish the staff of the little club all the best – but completely snubbed Allison. When Marcus Browning then grabbed a dramatic second-half equaliser to earn us a replay it got even more bitter. I think Atkinson refused to shake hands afterwards and certainly never went near our dressing-room. His number two Jim Barron tried to iron things out, but the feeling ran very deep. We lost the replay at Villa Park 3-0, and as far as I'm aware Big Ron and Big Mal never spoke a word to each other there either!

All that drama in the Cup, and the big headlines it created, hid the fact for a few weeks that our League results were going downhill again. And it wasn't long before Allison's reign was over.

In keeping with his image, Malcolm liked to socialise after games. He enjoyed a drop of red wine and a brandy, and being such a celebrity there was never a shortage of people to buy him a drink and keep his glass topped up. The wealthier fans who still made up the Presidents Club always enjoyed the company of such a larger than life figure. And once he'd shared a drink or two in there, and then walked into the boardroom for a glass of champagne, he would begin to become quite inebriated.

One of my duties was to get him back to his hotel in Keynsham, and if I didn't do the job then Jason the bar manager at Twerton Park would take charge. One night they were celebrating Jason's birthday and had both drunk more than their fair share. They got back to what they thought was the hotel – but unfortunately went to the wrong side of the road. Instead they spent hours hammering on the door of the church – which looks much like the hotel door and in their state probably looked identical – wondering why nobody would open up for them!

Anyway, the more he drank the more forthright his views would become. As results began to go the wrong way I suspect some of that honesty late at night in the boardroom backfired on him. Now whether he did say something after a few drinks to upset a director I don't know. But the top and bottom of it was that with 13 games still to go and the team bottom of the table again, the adventure with Malcolm Allison as Bristol Rovers manager was brought to a close. Steve Cross was given two games as caretaker – and then came the news that John Ward of York City was to be our next boss.

JOHN WARD – AND WEMBLEY AGAIN

W E weren't sure what was going to happen when Malcolm Allison left and Steve Cross took charge of the team for a game or two. There were all sorts of rumours about who might take over, and one morning Geoff Dunford appeared at the training ground with several of the other directors and Martin O'Neill alongside them.

At this time Martin, who has since established himself as one of Britain's top managers at Leicester and then Celtic, was an up and coming boss of ambitious Wycombe who were attempting to get out of the Vauxhall Conference and had built a superb new stadium. Our directors thought they could entice him with the chance to jump straight into the League, and the interview seemed to have gone well.

They introduced Martin to me, and we chatted about his days at Nottingham Forest with the great Brian Clough and shared a story or two about Miah Dennehy who had played alongside him before coming to Rovers in the 1980s. As we looked around the Portakabins Martin asked me: "Is this where you normally train?", and obviously I told him it was. He just said: "No, I don't think I could swop this for the luxury I have got at Wycombe." And that was the end of any hope of him coming to work for Rovers!

In the event it wasn't long after when Geoff Dunford arrived at the training ground again and this time introduced John Ward to us as the new manager. Within days Ward had hit the place like a whirlwind.

For all that Malcolm Allison's time had ended with the results falling away, he had definitely had an impact on the team. The standard of fitness was much higher, and I think the younger players in particular had begun to think in a more professional way about how they should look after themselves.

So John Ward moved that on again because he immediately set out to raise all the standards around the club. He was a new broom that began to sweep hard, and suddenly we found everything being painted and repaired. There were still 11 games to go and a relegation battle to be fought, but John wasn't interested in waiting until the end of the season to sort out the structure at the club. He obviously wasn't too impressed at finding four Portakabins as his base, but he was determined to get what facilities we did have upgraded.

Before he'd gone to York to become a manager in his own right he had been used to working with Graham Taylor at Aston Villa, and he wanted to aspire to those standards even if he knew we were still some way from achieving them.

John won his first home game 3-1 against Peterborough, but he needed to produce a sensational change in playing form immediately to have a chance of keeping us up and that was probably beyond anybody. But he did start to promote some of the youngsters and by the end of the season, when our fate was settled, was prepared to throw them into the first team.

Our last game of the campaign was at Millwall, and it was going to be a historic afternoon because it was the final match played after 83 years of history at The Den. It was rather tough for us to see that Millwall were preparing to move to a wonderful new stadium while we were still marooned at Twerton Park and searching in vain to find a site back in Bristol to call our own. But we would at least share a special day in another club's history, and knew they would be looking forward to a party.

Now Millwall has always been one of my least favourite places to play. Not because there's anything wrong with either the New Den or the old Den before it – it's simply I could never find a suitable place for the pre-match meal. All the hotels were either ridiculously expensive or too far away, and every year I seemed to try something different.

There was the period when Bobby Gould was in charge that we stopped the coach along the embankment for tea and toast. And I was still smarting from when a few years earlier I had made the worst booking ever.

I'd been told how Bristol City had been to the Tower hotel alongside the Tower of London, and been charged £17.50 each for beans on toast. That didn't exactly fit the Rovers budget, so I asked Millwall for a more economical recommendation. When they told me about "London Park Hotel", near to the Elephant and Castle, and I got quoted a very reasonable price I decided to book it. The name made it sound very prestigious.

We arrived on time at 11.45, and were shown into a pleasant entrance area before being told to go downstairs to the private room where our meal would be served. It probably couldn't have been more of a dungeon if we had gone to the Tower itself, with one waitress who was about 70 years old serving us, and a series of card tables covered in paper towels for us to eat off. It was the worst place I'd ever booked, and the lads never allowed me to forget it.

Anyway this year we'd stopped further out at the Post House by the Black Prince junction near Sidcup, and were met by the normal police escort as we drove closer to the ground. I went through my pre-match chores and everything was fine – although when the lads came back from warming up they were having a grumble or two. The groundsman had refused to let them go anywhere near the goalmouths at either end and had been very over zealous. Quite why he was so worried about protecting his pitch when it was about to be torn up by bulldozers I don't know! But then I've never met a groundsman yet who wasn't fussy about his patch of grass. I think they'd all be much happier if they could just get on and make it look beautiful and nobody ever actually played any games!

This was where we got the first look at John Ward's careful preparation and thoughtful qualities, as he wound the team up to ruin Millwall's day. He felt they were expected to just arrive and be beaten so the home fans could enjoy their final memories of their traditional home. And he was determined that wouldn't happen.

He gave a 20-year-old Bristol kid called Lee Archer his full debut, and an 18-year-old from Yate by the name of Mike Davies a chance on the bench. And both of them scored as we cruised to a 3-0 win. The Millwall fans were furious, and behind us a number of them were ripping up seating and throwing it at the back of the dug-out. I was more frightened than I have ever been in my life, and we needed the police to protect us as the final whistle went and we got off to the safety of the dressing-rooms.

The police wanted us to leave as soon as possible and we weren't too bothered about hanging around ourselves. But first we had to stop in the Old Kent Road where I had ordered our fish and chips for the journey back and it was the only time I can ever remember needing a police escort to go into a chip shop! Otherwise it could have been me and not the cod that got battered!

In the summer John did more to get things reorganised. Most important of all he brought in Dennis Booth to be his number two and they made a perfect pairing.

John was – and still is, come to that – a quiet, thorough and thoughtful person who didn't waste words. He would give a player a lift if he required it, but if anybody wanted knocking down he was a dab hand at that too. He'd normally only get irate if people did silly things – especially if they got bookings for daft stuff like kicking the ball away or arguing with referees. He was a first class ambassador himself and expected his players to conduct themselves in the same way. And while he might have kept his family home in Birmingham he committed himself totally to Bristol, coming down on Monday and staying all week until Saturday's game.

Dennis, who had been with John at Aston Villa, was a different kind of person again. He was a bundle of fun, full of energy with a big round jolly face that was never without a smile. He always had a joke to tell or a prank to play. So while the boss was serious and thought hard about training and tactics, his sidekick kept the atmosphere continually light and full of fun. On away trips he'd muck about with the coach driver, ruffling his hair and teasing him while the bus rattled down the motorway. Dennis simply couldn't keep quiet or still. The result was that the atmosphere among the players was always relaxed and happy, and that's good for team spirit.

Mind you, when it was time to be serious Dennis could do that too. He took a 21-year-old Marcus Stewart under his wing and encouraged him to come in for extra training each day. Marcus was finding it difficult to adjust to first team football after scoring a lot of goals for the reserves, and Dennis began to do an extra 30 minutes with him before training every morning, and then another hour or so in the afternoon too.

Dennis taught him how to control the ball on his chest, to use both his feet, and where to run and how to do all the physical things that centre-forwards have to do to unsettle a defender. He got him to think about what he was eating and drinking, and how to look after his body —and it's no surprise to me that Marcus has gone on to be near the top of the Premiership scoring charts with Ipswich. I'm sure he'd tell you himself how much he is in debt to Dennis Booth.

John began the season by selling Steve Yates to Queen's Park Rangers for £650,000, spending £140,000 of the money on winger Worrell Sterling. I was disappointed to see Yates go because he was the best YTS boy I ever worked with. That wasn't just because he helped me a lot, but because his attitude was fantastic. You only ever needed to tell him something once and it was done. He brought me a cut glass tankard as a going away present before he left to play in the Premier League, and that's also a very special part of my souvenir collection.

John's efforts to streamline the organisation of the club created yet another office move, with the administration staff all being transferred from the main office at Two Mile Hill to the ground floor of an office block at Fry's. It was a mammoth task for all concerned to move everything, but it did mean that we had the entire staff all under one roof.

There was a main boardroom with all our own gear and furniture, and as well as the offices for the administration and commercial staff we also created a club shop and ticket office. The players also had a section, along with John Ward's own office, and there was even space for the Youth and Community sections as well. It was great luxury, we thought – although the poor old kit man was still forced to stay in my Portakabin at the bottom of the field because they said I should be closer to the training and playing action!

Mind you, I certainly couldn't complain about things at the club after the chairman Denis Dunford and his directors awarded me a testimonial season as a reward for my loyal service. With the help of Bob Twyford I established a small committee of people to whom I will always be grateful – so here's an opportunity now to record my thanks to Bob, John Goodchild, Brian Harding, John Harding, Peter and John Thornell and Roy Cowell. We met once a month and they all worked so hard to make it a great success. We started with darts matches and race nights in pubs and clubs in the Bristol and Bath area, and also held a golf day at Mangotsfield. I must also mention Graham Bowen and his wonderful wife Sue for their great organisational skills at all these functions, especially when we went on to have a cabaret evening at Redwood Lodge with Eddie Large and former Everton player Duncan Campbell as the speakers. Many former players, directors and managers came from all over the country to give me wonderful support. And just as much an honour was the way the Bristol City directors and staff attended along with their president Marina Dolman who was a great friend of Jan Moules and myself.

That was a night I'll always remember – but it was followed then by my testimonial game at Twerton Park on 9 May 1994. It was incredible to have a match played for me by Bristol Rovers. Who would have believed it 44 years earlier when Ron Moules first chatted to me and asked if I fancied helping out at Eastville?

Bob Twyford had spoken to all sorts of clubs trying to arrange a fixture, and we had used Malcolm Allison too who tried his best endeavours with both Manchester United and Manchester City. They were all committed to different tours, and the man who came to help us instead was Bobby Gould who had gone back to manage Coventry a second time. It was brilliant that he got his chairman John Poynton to agree to bring the first team – but I then had another worry when Bobby parted company with the Sky Blues again. Thankfully Mr Poynton honoured the promise, and Phil Neal brought them to Twerton for a wonderful evening.

It rounded off a season that had shown great promise at one stage, with Ward's team hitting second place in the table at the end of February only to slip away when it mattered and end up in eighth place and just outside the play-off positions.

But by the time John went into his second full season, he had got things set up as he wanted them and it showed. He spent £100,000 on bringing Paul Miller in from Wimbledon as another forward, and suddenly we had a potent strike force. Apart from Miller – and a couple of longer serving lads like Andy Tillson and Justin Channing – the squad was made up of free transfers and bargain captures. And the team spirit shone through.

Marcus Stewart was reaping the benefit of all Dennis Booth's hard work, while Weston-super-Mare-born Gareth Taylor, picked up several years earlier from Southampton on a free transfer, also blossomed alongside Miller. I was thrilled for Gareth, who had recovered from cruciate ligament damage to his knee. It was the sort of injury which had almost always finished a player's career in the past, but the work which had been done to help Paul Gascoigne recover from his horrific injury after the 1991 FA Cup Final was being copied elsewhere. And not only medical science was improving but Rovers' own treatment of injuries was better. That was also down to John Ward who had brought in Keith James to be his physio, and the treatment was much more professional in the proper room which had been created in a basement of a building at Fry's. We lost just two of the last 18 games to clinch a play-off place, and on a long night at

Gresty Road, Paul Miller scored the goal in extra-time which took us to the final on the away goals rule.

We all went through every emotion as the prospect of another Wembley trip dawned, but this time I was determined to savour the big day. The first time it had flown by in a whirl, and this trip to the Twin Towers was one I wanted to relish.

Sure enough, I enjoyed the experience far more. Because you've already been there, you have less sense of wonderment and you get more chance to take it all in.

This time we stayed at the Post House at Beaconsfield, and again set off to Wembley wearing our smart new club blazers that the commercial department had arranged, with a motor-cycle escort to take us through the crowds. We had to change colours to wear our green and black away quarters, and it was terrific to see the amount of green and black flags in among all the blue.

I sat in the front of the coach for the journey, determined to enjoy every moment of the drive up Wembley Way and into those big gates, and once again more than 30,000 Bristolians swelled the crowd to the biggest ever for the Second Division play-off game.

John and Dennis had been adamant that every member of the football club staff should be there, and they looked so proud as they led the team out. I walked out behind our line of players, but even though I then had to turn right and go around the dog track my knees still went wobbly. I'm sure many players and managers have described the feeling as you emerge from that long tunnel into the bright sunlight of a Wembley afternoon and the wall of noise hits you. And most of them could describe it better than me. But if you're not a footballer, but just a fan from the back streets of Bristol who has been lucky enough to spend his life involved with your special club, the feeling is even more emotional because you can't believe how lucky you are to be there.

The game itself flew by, as Wembley matches do. We conceded a goal just before half-time but went straight back and Marcus Stewart equalised within seconds. Huddersfield's manager Neil Warnock – you'll remember we'd upset him by winning a Wembley place ahead of his Notts County team four years earlier – was furious with his players as we went back down the tunnel, not waiting until they got in the dressing-room to begin ranting and raving at how they had conceded the goal.

He was happy afterwards. We had the best of the second half, but couldn't get the goal we deserved and instead Chris Billy got the winner against the run of play nine minutes from the end.

After we had picked ourselves up from the disappointment and loaded all our gear on the coach I went across to the banqueting hall – and there met Tom Finney. I chatted to him for some time, and it was a strange feeling to be so disappointed at losing and yet thrilled out of my mind to meet one of my all-time heroes. I also chatted to Plymouth's chairman Dan Macauley who told me: "You have just seen my new manager for next season." A few weeks later Neil Warnock went to Plymouth, and however surprised anybody else might have been it wasn't a shock to me! It seemed amazing that he had obviously been lining up his next job in the same breath as winning promotion.

We didn't go to London this time, but instead returned to the Fry's training ground where a first class party had been laid on. Again every member of staff from both the playing and non-playing side were invited, and it went on late into the evening. And for me there was a rare bonus – no kit to wash the next day because all the players had been allowed to keep their own gear as a souvenir of the day!

There were more disappointments to come that summer. A plan to build a new stadium on Severnside collapsed because of planning problems with Bristol City Council. And then Dennis Booth was enticed away – ironically to become number two at Huddersfield to Brian Horton. They had obviously heard good things about Dennis while we were socialising at Wembley. And to be honest I think to this day that John Ward was never the same person again. He appointed Steve Cross as his new assistant, but I think he missed having the uplifting personality around that Dennis had given him and he found it much harder to keep things going.

We sold Gareth Taylor to Crystal Palace for £1.6m, but hardly any of that money went back into the team in terms of transfer fees. We also suffered from some serious injuries with the unlucky Justin Skinner breaking his leg.

It meant the team were younger and younger, and it showed when we got drawn away to non-League Hitchin in the FA Cup. You'd think we were used to bad conditions after nearly a decade at Twerton, but Hitchin was something else again – a pokey little ground. The dressing-rooms were terrible, like a wooden shed. And you could sense before the match that the attitude wasn't right.

Hitchin then had a few ex-pros who wanted to mix it a bit, and the upshot was that while some of our older players like Dave Pritchard got very aggressive some of the younger ones were intimidated and we finished up losing 2-1. The truth was we were outplayed and where our teams normally battled against the odds they just didn't have the spirit to handle the conditions.

As the season wore on we signed Peter Beadle from Watford for £30,000, and he produced enough goals to make sure that we at least stayed clear of trouble. I liked Peter, and the supporters did too once he scored two goals in two minutes to give us a victory at Ashton Gate in the derby match. I used to give him sweets and chocolates from the factory at Fry's to take home to his two sons and they were a lovely family.

By the end of the season there was encouraging news as we learned the years of travelling to Twerton were about to end thanks to a plan to move back to Bristol and share the Memorial Ground – just a mile or two up the road from our real home at Eastville.

But John Ward wasn't going to get the chance to share that adventure. He and Steve Cross were both told that their contracts would not be renewed at the end of the campaign. It was typical of John, though, that if he was going to leave the club he would do it in style. He had always taken us all out for lunch at Christmas time. And now together with his wife he invited the entire club again for a meal to say thank you for everything we had done.

OLLIE AND BACK TO BRISTOL

I N all the years I was involved at Bristol Rovers I don't think I ever met another player or manager so consistently and compellingly enthusiastic as Ian Holloway. And that wasn't just when he became a pro, or when he got to take over the club he had supported as a boy. He was like it from the moment I first encountered him at the age of eight.

I must have seen hordes of kids who came and went during the time that Rovers ran the Parkway scheme, and hundreds of young boys appeared at different times to play for us, all dreaming of becoming professional footballers. I'd remember a few of them, but Ollie, as he was known by one and all from the first time I met him, stuck out above them all. His father Bill, a good local player, was involved in running one of the Parkway teams and had shown great enthusiasm, and so it wasn't difficult to see where Ian got his character from.

As the tiniest kid Ollie had a massive force of personality. If he wasn't chosen to play for a team and had to be substitute he'd pester the life out of the manager until he got on. And while most of the kids just came, played and went home again, Ollie would hang around asking questions and wanting to learn everything about the way the club was run.

When he then became an apprentice he wanted to practice, learn and improve all the time. And he passionately believed in his own ability. I've already mentioned how he moaned at the arrival of Alan Ball during Bobby Gould's first spell in charge, and was furious that he was losing his first team place even if it was to a legend. It didn't matter that Alan Ball had a World Cup winner's medal in his pocket and 72 England caps. Ian was convinced he was better. Meanwhile Bobby just kept telling him to watch and learn – and he did.

Ollie had also learned from his time away from the club at Wimbledon and Brentford, and again from playing under Gerry Francis in the 1990 Championship side. When Gerry took him off to Queen's Park Rangers to play for five years in the Premiership he was alongside Ray Wilkins and got another side to his education.

Now that same enthusiasm and passion for his favourite club was exactly what Rovers needed as they prepared to return to Bristol and move into the Memorial Ground.

I don't think Ollie had been first choice for the job. There were all sorts of rumours about what might happen, including a third spell in charge for Bobby Gould. But he'd prepared himself carefully for his interview and had a plan written out for the future and how he saw the club developing. He had a dream that Bristol Rovers could become a much bigger club, and superbly set out his hopes and ideas.

As soon as Ollie came that same energy was put into the staff. He told us the club must be more professional, and our attitude had to improve. And he told me that the years of scrimping and saving over kit must end and he wanted things done properly irrespective of the cost. He was determined to make us feel proud to be Bristol Rovers, and even covered up all the fire extinguishers because he didn't want anything red around the camp! He went around the club bringing in bunches of flowers for the backroom staff – people like the office manager Angela Mann and the Commercial Department's assistant

Eve O'Reilly who worked long hours with great commitment and weren't always recognised. Ollie wanted them to feel part of the team.

He also wanted old fashioned discipline and laid down a far more regimented code of conduct than we'd been used to while John Ward was in charge. That's no disrespect to John because every manager has their own different style. But all in all it created a good atmosphere and was a refreshing new start for a club that was in the process of changing in other ways.

The most important difference, of course, was that we had a new home ground. And to be moving back to Bristol after ten years at Bath was a special step forward. Okay, it wasn't the new, purpose built all-seater stadium about which we had dreamed since that amazing night when Gordon Bennett turned up with a furniture van to move us out of Eastville. But compared to Twerton Park it was luxury, especially once the dressing-rooms in the new West Stand were completed within a few weeks of our move. After years of squeezing into a tiny space we could now spread ourselves around a giant room that had been designed to cope with a 21-man Rugby Union squad, and had a huge plunge bath as well as a suite of showers. Just luxury!

My matchday routine was so much easier without the need of a 12-mile trek to Bath, that was for sure. I could collect all the stuff from the training ground at Fry's at nine in the morning, go back to the stadium to lay it out around the dressing-room, and then pop back home to my flat in Westbury to have a shower and change before reporting again for duty at 12 noon.

Sadly it wasn't long before Ollie discovered the first problem of being a manager in these modern times – trying to keep a player who wants to move. Dennis Booth had convinced his boss at Huddersfield Brian Horton to put in a bid of more than £1million for Marcus Stewart, and the player wanted to go. In fairness Marcus had blossomed by this time into a superb player and felt it was time to move on and test his talent higher up the League.

But Ollie tried everything to keep him. He offered huge amounts of money, and even produced a gleaming new car that would be for

Marcus if he'd only sign a new contract. Together with Geoff Twentyman who had returned to the club as Ian's number two they spent hours trying to sell him their dream of what Rovers could achieve.

I think it shook Ollie that Marcus was still so determined to go. It was his first taste of the reality of the job, which is that you can't keep an unhappy player. Back in the old days of the 1950s when we had the "no buy, no sell" rule the club was in charge – but now the power was in the dressing-room.

Ollie's answer was to sign Jamie Cureton from Norwich for £250,000, and together with Peter Beadle they picked up enough goals to keep us in the middle of the table – although we did have a bit of a relegation scare for a while. That was when we signed a big, awkward lad from Halesowen called Julian Alsop. He had been playing non-League football while humping bricks around a building site for a living, and his enthusiasm at suddenly getting the chance to play full time rubbed off on the other players. I think that possibly convinced Ian that the non-League ranks would be a good place to go on looking for new signings.

Meanwhile we had undergone yet another change of training ground, leaving behind the fields of Fry's to go to The Beeches in the grounds of a huge old house in Brislington which had been acquired by Geoff Dunford's companies from British Gas.

It meant another set of Portakabins to occupy – although it wouldn't be more than a year or so before we had purpose built changing rooms that were complete luxury. But there was another problem in store for the kit man because the pitches were all on a soil of red clay.

Before we moved Geoff Dunford warned me not to start grumbling about it. "There will be nothing you or I can do about it," he said. But I couldn't imagine just how hard it was going to make things. Within 20 minutes of the start of any training session when it was raining, every item of clothing that anybody was wearing would be red. It was embarrassing when we played youth or practice games. I remember Tottenham lining up for a match wearing all white, and by the time the game was over they looked more like Liverpool than Spurs! The Lilywhites had become the Reds! The problem was that however hard you tried you could never wash the colour out, either. We had every expert from every detergent company down there at one time or another, and nobody could find a solution. I was only grateful that Ollie at least maintained the rule that players had to take their own training gear home to wash!

There was another change due to make a kit manager's life more difficult when the League decided to follow the Premiership example and introduce squad numbers and names. It's a great idea for the fans, but what a headache for me! All of a sudden it meant I needed to take EVERY shirt to EVERY game. You couldn't afford for the manager to make a late change to his team and find the player in question's kit was miles away. We always take long and short sleeves for every player, so you are talking about 60 shirts which are always hung on a rail in numerical order while you wait for the manager to name his squad. When there's a new player signed 24 hours before kick-off it requires even more running around to get a shirt named and numbered in time! On one occasion I had to thank Oldham's Commercial Department for using their machine to name and number a shirt for me just two hours before kick-off.

Throughout that first season Ollie was a player-manager, and was probably our best player in nine games out of ten. He led by example, although his enthusiasm got him carried away at times and his disciplinary record wasn't good. He'd shout and bawl at the players and at the referee too if he thought there was an injustice. There's no doubt that the different pressures of organising and getting your own performance right makes being a player-manager the most difficult job in football (after the kit manager, of course!).

His second season began with a double signing from non-League football – Barry Hayles and Steve Foster. And that too was a good example of Ollie's enthusiastic mind.

He had been keeping track of Hayles who was scoring goals for fun for Stevenage in the Conference, and had virtually decided to sign him when he went to watch him play once more for luck.

Together with Gary Penrice, who would later join his management team but at that time was still playing for Watford, he took in a match against Woking.

Hayles had a nightmare, and Ollie was just beginning to decide that perhaps he might save his money when it occurred to them both why the striker they fancied so strongly was doing so badly. The centre-half he was facing – Foster – was having an outstanding game. So they took the brave decision to sign both players and immediately had the backbone of their next season's team.

While Foster grew in confidence at the back, Hayles burst into the team with three goals in the first three matches and never stopped scoring all season. He got 23 in the League, and two more in the Cup, while Beadle weighed in with 17 and Cureton picked up 13. It meant Alsop, whose impact a year earlier had probably saved us getting into relegation trouble, was surplus to requirements – and the £15,000 fee that Swansea paid for him was used to buy a minibus for the youth and reserve team. That was another example of how Ollie was trying to build every aspect of the club. A decent van was more important to him than an average centre-forward! Yet again it was an example of his desire to improve the club's image and build more than just a team.

The season had its hiccups. We lost 3-0 at Wigan on a frosty pitch in December and had FOUR players sent off. Dave Pritchard, Jason Perry, Andy Tillson and Josh Low all got their marching orders simply for mistimed tackled in the conditions. We ended up with just seven players on the field and the only blessing was that Ollie kept his temper in check enough not to join the red card queue!

If Ollie had a fault – which was also a strength in some ways – it was that he couldn't tolerate mistakes. He set himself the highest standards and he expected everybody else to do the same. It was probably why he always chopped and changed his team so much – using 29 players in both his first two seasons. And if he wasn't happy with somebody's attitude then he quickly dumped them from his plans.

Andy Collett, our goalkeeper, was one who suffered for that. Andy was quite a decent keeper but was a very cocky young lad. He used to label himself "The Number One", and even signed autographs by writing down "The Number One Keeper" instead of his name. Incidentally the rules were that because of the mud the goalkeepers were the only ones who didn't have to wash their own training gear, and Andy used to try to take advantage by putting other dirty clothes in among his training kit to try to get them cleaned as well! In the end it cost him because Ollie fell out with him over his attitude and went to Swansea to sign Lee Jones in his place.

If Ollie's first season had been about survival, this second campaign was a different matter. At one point in January we stitched five straight wins together to go third in the table, and then after falling away a bit hit another run of 13 points from 15. On 2 May, Cureton and Hayles got a goal each against Brentford in front of our biggest home crowd yet of 9,043 and we were back in the play-offs.

We smashed Northampton 3-1 at home in the first leg, and I think everybody believed we were more than half way to Wembley. But when we got to Sixfields, the smart new ground that Northampton now occupy, we had a shock.

Northampton's manager Ian Atkins had clearly been influenced by his time at Cambridge under John Beck. The same tactics of hustle and bustle were being used, and they began even before we got on the field. As the teams lined up to go out together there were all sorts of verbals going on in the tunnel. Their coach Garry Thompson who had played with Ollie at QPR didn't like the fact that Rovers thought they were already through and had got their players full of fury. Quite simply we got battered in the game as well, and couldn't stand up to the hustle and bustle. Ollie himself was suspended from playing in both legs, and without him on the field we didn't have the character to compete. We lost 3-0, and the promotion dream was gone. You could sum up what happened in one word. Intimidation. But what a great experience it had been.

It still hit Ian hard, and he shook up his staff again by promoting Gary Penrice to be his assistant and then going back to Northampton to entice Thompson away. That was a good move because Garry expresses himself very well, is full of the same sort of enthusiasm that

Ollie has, and he immediately began to work wonders with some of the younger players.

Among them was Jason Roberts, who had been bought from Wolves where he was in their reserves. And I have to say he was going to blossom into one of the best centre-forwards I've seen at Bristol Rovers in all my 51 years. It's a personal opinion, and I'm sure other people would think I'm mad, but when Robbo is on song I think he's a colossus. He's right up in the same class as Geoff Bradford and Alfie Biggs in my view, and is as good as any we've ever had. I loved his bubbly character off the field, and his arrogance and cockiness off it. And just like Marcus Stewart before him he had an appetite for work. He regularly came in half an hour early to practice on his own or have individual coaching from Gary Penrice or Garry Thompson and it was no wonder he kept improving.

Probably the most significant thing that happened that year, however, was that the old Bristol Rugby club went bust. They had just simply failed to cope with the switch to professional Rugby Union. And thanks to a clause or two in the contract which Geoff Dunford had skilfully negotiated a few years earlier the football club now became owners of the ground. More than 50 years after that ill-fated decision to sell Eastville for £12,000, Bristol Rovers at last owned their own home.

It took Roberts half of that first season to find his feet with only one goal before November, but once he started scoring he couldn't stop. It meant we could sell Barry Hayles to Fulham for £2million and Roberts along with Jamie Cureton became the first choice partnership.

They had a natural instinct for playing together. At Reading Jamie got four and Robbo two as we won 6-0, and at Stoke they shared three goals again in a 4-1 win. That was an odd game. Our board had refused to sit in the directors box in a protest because Stoke had reduced the prices for their own fans but charged the Rovers fans full price. And after the game the police horses were brought on to keep the home fans off the pitch because they were protesting at Brian Little's management. (He lost his job soon after, incidentally).

We had a good run in the FA Cup too, until losing at Barnsley in the fifth round. And you could see the signs of a new team coming together, especially after the signings of Andy Thomson, Robbie Pethick and Dave Hillier from Portsmouth. They had all fallen foul of the arrival of Alan Ball as manager.

We also, incidentally, brought in another goalkeeper to give Lee Jones some competition. Michel Kuipers had been a commando in the Dutch army, and was a likeable lad with a fabulous physique. He could pick up the metal skips that I kept the kit in with two hands as if they were just matchboxes. Unfortunately he wasn't so successful as a goalkeeper, and his only game at Bournemouth was a disaster. Somehow we only lost 1-0, but his kicking was hopeless – every time he hit the ball it was like a golfer with a bad slice!

By the start of the 1999-2000 season Ollie had a settled side for probably the first time. And it showed in the results as Roberts and Cureton got the goals and the rest of the team looked totally solid. We had lost only three times by the middle of November, and then we brought in Mark Walters from Swindon on a free transfer to add a new dimension to it all.

Mark had done it all in the game, and still had wonderful skill to go past a defender and then a fabulous ability to cross the ball. He also brought a charming personality with no edge at all, and we won 10 of the next 12 games to go top of the League. The winning roll started, incidentally, at Chesterfield where Dave Pritchard scored the first goal of his Rovers career. A young fan called Ben Davies had told his mates a few months earlier that if Pritchard ever scored a goal in an away game he'd walk home. Fair play to the lad because he was as good as his word. When Chesterfield came to play us in March, young Ben, together with some friends, spent the week before walking every step of the way from Saltergate to the Memorial Stadium and arrived just in time for kick-off. They raised around £3,000 for cancer charities and to help fund the roof being built above the Family Terrace at the Stadium. The supporters club had already helped finance a roof above the terrace at one end so the fans could at least stand out of the rain. While other clubs were building modern, all-seater stadiums it was a small step forward. But for us it was like luxury!

That 3-1 win at home to Chesterfield on 18 March kept us in second place and opened up a nine-point gap from third. It seemed surely we would at last return to the second level of English football, and this time the club might be better equipped to stay there.

But then came the crash. We took just six points from the last 10 games and didn't even get into the play-offs. And to this day I don't think anybody completely understands why.

Certainly the injuries to Ronnie Mauge and Dave Pritchard were significant. Ronnie had come to us from Plymouth and was an aggressive, tigerish midfield man who was a good organiser on and off the field. His progress won him a chance to play international football for Trinidad and Tobago – and he came back with a horrible bad break to his leg. Pritchard had knee trouble. And it didn't help either that 17-year-old Simon Bryant, who had been given his chance by Ollie, was also suffering from injury. We didn't have a strong midfield man to win the ball.

Beyond that I think you also have to question the tactics we used. I say that with all respect to Ollie because he'll know more about football than I ever will. But he did chop and change the way he wanted us to play during that last spell, and some of the players were never quite sure what they should be doing. Having said that, it was their fault and not the manager's that some of them reacted by putting in a good deal less effort than they'd done before. We reached the lowest point at Cardiff on the final day of the season when the performance was abysmal. We had finished seventh when we could have been champions. The air in the dressing-room was blue. There were rows, things thrown around in temper, yet oddly silences too because we were in a state of great shock. I don't think anybody could understand why we had so under performed at the end of what had been a very good season. Yet if you think back to Bert Tann's era even his sides suffered the same sort of thing when the pressure built. It is something that happens in football, although I don't think anybody quite knows why.

TIME TO GO

NOBODY believed it when I told them, but I decided it was time for me to go. I was 70 years old, and beginning to feel that I simply couldn't get all the kit around like I used to. I decided that when my 71st birthday came on 28 October 2000, I would retire.

I'd been there so long that not many people felt I could stop working. But I'd made up my mind and stuck to it. Although some of the things that happened before I went were unbelievable.

First we had a pre-season tour to Ireland. I'd finally got my trip into Europe! We flew from Bristol with all the kit packed into 12 huge metal boxes, and reached our base at the beautiful hotel at Portmarnock, right on the coast just north of Dublin.

In previous years – and particularly when John Ward was in charge – we had been to the Isle of Wight in pre-season. I always felt it was good to get the lads away together and build team spirit. And this year it was just as valuable because the atmosphere after the disappointment of missing out on promotion was low.

Jason Roberts didn't come because he was on his way to West Bromwich Albion. Jamie Cureton was also trying to get away and had made it clear he didn't want to stay.

So it was good that the players we did have could share some laughs on tour. At two of the tiny grounds where we played we couldn't get the coach anywhere near the dressing-rooms. And at another we arrived at the wrong place because our Irish hosts had changed the venue but forgotten to tell us! But when all these problems were resolved we sure got a wonderful friendly Irish welcome wherever we went in glorious sunshine.

On the way home Roger Brinsford, the secretary, and I did the checking in job in reverse, and all the metal skips were loaded on to the flight. Unfortunately when we landed in Bristol we discovered that we had exceeded the weight limits, so the other personal baggage had been left behind for another flight the following day! At least half the lads therefore had no car keys, and we had a quick job to organise ways to get everybody safely back home. The bags did eventually turn up – but not until the next afternoon! In their gloriously laid back way the Irish had completely forgotten to tell us about it!

The season seemed to start well enough. We had a spectacular night in the rain when we knocked Everton out of the Worthington Cup on penalties, and then only narrowly lost to Sunderland in the next round. And until we went to Bury on 6 October we were unbeaten.

And we could still have some fun. A few days later we lost at home to Northampton, and in the boardroom afterwards the mood was glum. I decided to give the directors a lift by performing a silly dance. I think it is called a Sun Dance, with all the movements ultra slow. The mood picked up, and they all said there and then they would do the same in a cabaret act for me when I had my retirement party at The Beeches.

I never thought any more of it, but sure enough as the end of October approached we all went to practise a Wilson, Kappel and Betty type routine. Barry Bradshaw's wife Shirley and Geoff Dunford's partner Sharon put us through our paces, and all the directors except Vernon Stokes who pleaded a bad knee joined in on the night. We wore long night shirts and fezzes, with false moustaches and sunglasses – although for some reason my nightshirt was a mini-skirt length and was up around my Y-fronts! It made a spectacular entertainment for my retirement party, and I can't think the same thing would happen among the directors at any other club in the

League! It might sound silly, but it was just great and gave a superb laugh and a wonderful final send-off.

Just like my big days at Wembley, my retirement day went so quickly. And although I have carried on with my match day jobs looking after the visiting directors in the boardroom, and have been invited to travel away and help the new kit man James Brown to settle in, it has still been strange to see the club from outside.

There have been some major shocks. I was so disappointed for Ollie when he lost his job early in January. I think the pressure caught up with him, and certainly after the bitter disappointment of his promotion campaign falling apart I don't think he was the same person. It's funny how people can be changed by events. Just as John Ward suffered from losing Dennis Booth as his right hand man, so I don't think Ollie got over the fact that he had not managed to deliver his dream. He wasn't the same bubbly, enthusiastic person he had been before. I guess pressure gets to us all at some time in life, but I will always owe a debt of thanks to Ollie for all his kindness and help down the years I've known him – and also to his lovely wife Kim and their family for such true friendship.

The biggest shock of all was for the club to be relegated. And if there's a sad moment to completing this history it is that I have to record the club playing in the bottom level of the League for the first time ever. I was sad for Garry Thompson, who worked so hard to turn things round after Ollie left but somehow the fates always seemed to conspire against him. Maybe some of the referees didn't help either. We seemed to suffer a run of ridiculous decisions that cost vital points.

I was on holiday in Turkey on the night Rovers went down. I'd gone away believing we were sure to win at least two of three home games in a week and that should keep us safe. Instead we lost first to Port Vale and then Wycombe. I had the scores faxed to me at my hotel in Ishmelere, and just sat stunned as I took in the full implications.

With Gerry Francis returning for a second spell in charge, I'm sure Rovers will be back. And I'm sure I'll still be around the club for a good few years to watch them. I just hope my good health, which is the most priceless thing we all have, will keep me ticking over to see us make the rapid return up the Leagues which all Rovers followers everywhere want for this wonderful club.

POSTSCRIPT

IT seems amazing that a chance meeting at a cricket match more than 50 years ago could have changed my life so much. Going through my story, and the story of the club, has given me a wonderful reminder of how lucky I have been.

There are so many people to whom I owe a thank you, starting with the wonderful Ron Moules and his wife Jan who encouraged me to help out at the Rovers in the first place. If I try to mention them all by name I'm bound to miss somebody out, and the list would be so long it would be boring.

So I'll just record my thanks to every chairman, director, manager and secretary that I've known down the years. To all the members of Rovers' playing and administration staff, to the Presidents Club and Season ticket holders – and all the fans for their great friendship towards me as a person over all the many years.

Football, and Bristol Rovers, has brought me fun and excitement as well as occasional heartbreaks and disappointment. But more than that it has brought me deep friendships among players, managers, coaches, directors and supporters alike.

To all of them I wish good health and happiness, and more great enjoyment at Bristol Rovers Football Club.

Sincerely

Ray Kendall

INDEX